Shhh...

The Devil Is Listening

PAMELA MCKINNEY

DR. NES INTERNATIONAL CONSULTING & PUBLISHING

LOS ANGELES COUNTY, CA

Copyright © 2019 Shhh…The Devil is Listening by Pamela McKinney.

All rights reserved.

Dr. Nes International Consulting & Publishing
P.O. Box 70167
Pasadena, CA 91117
www.drnesintl.com

All rights reserved. No parts of this publication may be reproduced, stored in a retrieval system, or transmitted in any form or by any means—for example, electronic, photocopy, recording—without the prior written permissions of the author and/or publisher. The only exception is brief quotations in printed reviews.

At times, graphic in nature, this book recounts certain events in the life of Pamela McKinney according to her recollection and perspective. The purpose of this book is not to defame, but to empower and motivate readers to face their challenges despite of pain.

Editorial Work: Kia Stokes, M.B.A.
Cover Design: Jessica Land

ISBN: 978-1-949461-08-4

Shhh...The Devil is Listening

DEDICATION

I dedicate this book to all the people that have ever had to deal with any kind of abuse and felt alone. Abuse can leave a big empty hole in your heart and your mind full of confusion. Uncertainties often creep in, but I want you to know that you can find strength in God to keep standing.

If you or anyone that you know is being abused, raped, or molested seek help immediately. Please do not feel like you are by yourself and you are the only one that this is happening to because this is not true. Please don't be ashamed. There are many waiting to help! Speak up!

PAMELA MCKINNEY

Blank pages are intentional

Shhh...The Devil is Listening

ACKNOWLEGDEMENTS

I want to thank both of my grandmothers: Ms. Sadie Nell Blakmore and Mrs. Luevada McKinney. They told me at a very young age that no matter how many times the enemy knocks me down, to get back up. They told me that no matter what, never ever stop calling on the name of Jesus. In the midst of every fight He will never leave you. When it seems like the enemy is winning and you are too weak to call out, just wave your hand.

I would like to acknowledge one of my street mothers, Ms. Etho May (Effie May). She opened her doors to me not considering my troubled pass. Thank you for letting me know that God loves a sinner as well as he loves a saint. I want to sincerely thank you for letting God show you the best in me even though my spirit was dead. Thanks for teaching me that prayers have power when they come from the heart. You gave me a glimmer of hope when you told me that one day God would save me no matter how broken and lost, I was. Your presence made a difference in my life.

Also, thank you to my second Street Mom, Ms. Odella. She was known to us as Mom's. Mom's, thank you for showing me how to survive the streets and how to never lose anymore of myself as a woman. You showed me how to become a woman of strength, courage, power, beauty, and a woman that forgives. You taught me to apologize. You allowed me to see myself as a woman with dreams, visions, peace and a sound mind. The most significant thing you taught me is no matter what I went through in my life, God had a purpose for all the good, the bad and most definitely the ugly things that happened to me. I love you Mom's and thank you for loving me during my deep sin and pain.

Finally, I want to recognize and thank God for all that He is and has been to me. I was bent down, broken and my soul was lost headed straight to hell. Lord, I didn't love you and I didn't even believe you loved me in return. In fact, the word love had been taken from my vocabulary and the feeling of love was beaten out of my heart and replaced with hatred and unforgiveness. My mind was set on making everyone around me experience the pain I felt and by making their lives a living hell. I was on a set mission to self-destruct. Then one day, out of sheer desperation, I screamed these words to the Lord, "I'm tired of being imprisoned and I need your help. Please help me!" And just like that, you saved me! I want to say thank you for letting me live to share my story.

~  Pamela McKinney

PAMELA MCKINNEY

TABLE OF CONTENTS

CHAPTER 1: *THE FUSS* 9

CHAPTER 2: *THE FIRE* 17

CHAPTER 3: *THE FAMILY* 37

CHAPTER 4: *THE FIGHT* 63

CHAPTER 5: *THE FAITH* 93

CHAPTER 6: *THE FORMATION* 111

CHAPTER 7: *THE FORGIVING* 115

FINAL NOTE 121

NOTES 123

CONTACT THE AUTHOR 129

PAMELA MCKINNEY

EZEKIEL 16:4-13 NIV

4 On the day you were born your cord was not cut, nor were you washed with water to make you clean, nor were you rubbed with salt or wrapped in cloths.

5 No one looked on you with pity or had compassion enough to do any of these things for you. Rather, you were thrown out into the open field, for on the day you were born you were despised.

6 "'Then I passed by and saw you kicking about in your blood, and as you lay there in your blood, I said to you, "Live!"[a]

7 I made you grow like a plant of the field. You grew and developed and entered puberty. Your breasts had formed, and your hair had grown, yet you were stark naked.

8 "'Later I passed by, and when I looked at you and saw that you were old enough for love, I spread the corner of my garment over you and covered your naked body. I gave you my solemn oath and entered into a covenant with you, declares the Sovereign Lord, and you became mine.

9 "'I bathed you with water and washed the blood from you and put ointments on you.

10 I clothed you with an embroidered dress and put sandals of fine leather on you. I dressed you in fine linen and covered you with costly garments.

11 I adorned you with jewelry: I put bracelets on your arms and a necklace around your neck,

12 and I put a ring on your nose, earrings on your ears and a beautiful crown on your head.

13 So you were adorned with gold and silver; your clothes were of fine linen and costly fabric and embroidered cloth. Your food was honey, olive oil and the finest flour. You became very beautiful and rose to be a queen.

Shhh...The Devil is Listening

1

THE FUSS

There is much in the media concerning the #METOO movement. From alleged stories about pop sensation Michael Jackson and R & B singer Robert Kelly, every time the television is powered up, there's a new story about the allegations of a teacher, priest or a coach and his or her abuse towards children in their care. Much of what is heard is not a new phenomenon. The fuss of sexual indiscretions has long been a practice for centuries. However, I don't believe many understand the impact of how the "fuss" can frustrate the future of many children.

Let me explain.

I wrote this next section and use it when I travel to speak about the fuss. When I began to learn about the impact of what it meant to be molested, here's what came to mind.

"MOLESTATION! It has so much power that it can hold so many of us in captivity for years and make it seems as if there is no way out. To a survivor, the word "molested means that we were tried and found guilty of a crime that we did not commit and put in prison where only the victims can see the invisible bars. Caged in our own minds with the constant rewinding and replaying of what happened to us, we are left trying to survive.

In this prison, we do not look forward to having many visits because the visitors that come to see us are the demons that constantly remind us of what was done to us. They remind us that we are going to die in our own blood in this prison that is designed especially for us.

You see, in this prison, the only music we ever get to hear is our own screams of our spirits being murdered every single day over and over again. You see, in this prison that holds us so very tight, the only thing you can do is hope and pray that maybe one day, someone will come by and take the screaming out of our head and the taste of our blood out of our mouth. And maybe, if we are blessed enough, this death sentence will be taken off our life.

You see, the word "molested" is taken so lightly that it has become meaningless to some people. But what they do not know is that molestation takes so much from you that sometimes it becomes unbearable. Some people have taken their own life because they felt trapped and didn't think that they had an escape route. The other route that some of us take is turning to drugs to escape the rated X images and the horror we had to endure from being "molested". You see the movie that we have to watch over and over in our heads in which we were the main characters of, we did not audition for. The part was forced upon us with no questions asked.

"Molested" is the name of our movie. The characters in this movie are unknown because he chooses his victims and he does not discriminate. No one in this movie will know if the molester is going to let you live or die. When you are young and you do not know God yet, you think your life is in his hands and whether you live or die is up to the violator. When it is just you and your molester, he becomes your master and he makes all the decisions concerning your life. When the horror movie is finally over and the molester is done devouring you, you are left drowning in your own blood. What many people do not know is that when he leaves, he takes so much of you with him. Some of the things he leaves with, you will never be able to get back. Things like your virginity, your childhood, your innocence, and everything that was once so pure is now all gone and never to be returned to you. He takes your smile away, your trust, the love you once felt and, in your mind, he has even taken your future. You will also lose your soul to him. In some cases, he can also take the ability away from you to ever be able to bare children, which once belonged to you.

Now, because his intentions were meant to destroy you, he had to leave you with something so that you would always remember him, and he could still control you from a distance and keep you in bondage.

These are the things your molester will leave just for you: anxiety, shame, depression, emptiness, suicidal thoughts, bitterness, hatred, hardened heart, hopelessness, fear, not wanting to love, not trusting anyone or anything, dead on the inside, nightmares, lost soul, in bondage, no faith and brokenness.

Men and women of God, when you hear someone say I was

molested, what they are actually saying is, "I was captured and put into the belly of the beast, and I survived. I may have been broken, but God did not let me be destroyed."

While graphic and intense, this book will give you a candid look into my journey in overcoming molestation. It is not meant to detest and disgust the reader, but instead to enlighten, in ways that many writers have not taken time to reveal. Buckle up for this ride!

2 Corinthians 4:8-9

8 [We are] troubled on every side, yet not distressed; [we are] perplexed, but not in despair;
9 Persecuted, but not forsaken; cast down, but not destroyed;

See, I should be dead. My people should have held my funeral at least 25 years ago. No really, it's a fact! There is NO way, I should be here to tell you this story. My life should have long been over! I should have died from the cigarette burns that incinerated my vagina when I was 5. I should not have survived the senseless violence with the countless number of gang affiliations. I should have been taken out after the overdose. I should have died after the intense surgical infections. THERE IS NO WAY I should have survived! NONE.

However, I was able to somehow limp away from the confusion and disgust of my past, and gasp for enough air to journal my story. I want to share with you some critical lessons and blessings from my journey. If you or someone you may know has ever faced a pain so deep it numbs you, I want you to take some time to read this book. You are not alone! And while much of what I experienced is complex and sometimes difficult to put into words, my message is simple: With God, you can make it to the other side of defeat!

When Paul opens in 2 Corinthians chapter 4, he does so after suffering great pain and loss. The text speaks of the possibility to survive despite the obstacles that the Apostles faced during biblical days. And while you, like me have probably experienced your share of hardships, I want you to know, no matter what you have experienced, you have potential to overcome! The very fact that you are here reading this book is a telltale sign that God is up to something major in your life. The fact that you are on the other side of what happened to you, what was done to you, is a major indication that you have a story and that you are a victor. Most days don't feel like a victory, but I want you to know that victory is not a location, a destination, or based on feelings. **Victory is knowing in your heart, mind and spirit that what came to kill me, lost its fight!**

Shhh...The Devil is Listening

This means, if you've lived to tell anybody about any part of your story, you too have the power to heal! No matter how you feel about what you've experienced, there is victory in knowing what was meant to kill you was a dud. There's a reason for pain not defeating you. My pain came to shut me up and shut me down. But just recently, I refused to allow it, so I wrote this book!

It might be a while before you can embrace the fullness of what I'm discussing here. That's fine. It's a process. For now, let me share a bit about my own road towards healing.

I want to forewarn you that I will lay out some very graphic scenes about the truth of my story. Everything from abuse and molestation, to drug usage and gang affiliations, to being ostracized and misunderstood. I take you on a tour of the truth about hurt, pain, dominance and control that has ultimately led to my journey towards healing. I tell this story not for you to feel pity for me, yet to inspire you. I want to remind you that what happened to you has more to do with the millions you will help, than anything else! Whether you have experienced rape, molestation, or another horrific act, what you experienced is about the people you will help. There are many that would have died in what you experienced. The pain thought it left you for dead, but your survival has to be celebrated by sharing. That's exactly what I aim to do here. I have been silent for decades, but today I want to share with you my truth.

For parents, we must remain watchful and engage in tough talks with our children regularly. My aim is not to blame, but to help parents learn of the warning signs of abuse. With extreme watchfulness, we can prevent stories of abuse, through constant conversations and engagement one family at a time.

2

THE FIRE

June 25, 2012 is a day forever etched in my mind. In fact, it was the day that changed my life in a very real way. This was the day that I lost my family. I lost my peace. I lost my sanity. I lost the only person that truly loved me. I lost ME!

It's crazy though, because I never knew out of such an intense loss, I would experience any kind of gain.

Let me explain.

I was never able to have children of my own (for reasons we will discuss at length later), but my husband had one daughter.

Originally, their relationship was strained because my husband never really put forth an effort to have a close bond or a relationship with his daughter. However, when his daughter became pregnant, she wanted her children to have a relationship with their grandparents. Once we learned of the pregnancy, we all grew a bit closer. At 21, she gave birth to our first grandson. We were elated to learn that he would soon become a staple in our lives. Truthfully, it was his birth that caused me to experience true love for the first time. It was the first time I ever felt wanted, needed and loved. He made me feel needed for the first time in my life. He was so connected to me. He would hold on to my finger tightly. He needed me. I was desperate to find a way to return an even stronger love to him.

When I first got married, we never owned a Christmas tree. I always associated having a Christmas tree with children. I never desired a Christmas tree because I never had children, but I always wondered what that would feel like. Though our grandson was still an infant, I remember wanting to make Christmas special for him, so I got a Christmas tree. It was so tall I had to stand on the ladder in order to place the topper on the tree. It was all surreal.

Shhh...The Devil is Listening

The love he exuded was pure, and he quickly became my pride and joy! I had never experienced a love like this before. He would hold onto my finger so tightly and look at me. He needed me and I soon learned that I needed him!

As I began to fall in love with our grandson, slowly my walls would come down to actually receive his love. However, there were occasions where our daughter would get angry with us and she would take the baby and stay away for a while.

Our daughter did not realize she was dealing with an abused person. I could emotionally disconnect rather quickly. However, this time I didn't. Soon we learned our daughter was on drugs and later we discovered she was twisted up in a situation involving a dope dealer. During this hassle, our daughter left our grandson alone in a parking lot as she ran to save her own life. We received a call to come to the location. Once we arrived, we learned the details of the situation. I was well aware of the streets and knew how things went. With this knowledge, I asked the dealers to transfer the bounty to me instead of my daughter. I worked tirelessly to pay off the debt that our daughter owed to them. Eventually, the courts granted us full custody of her son, Day'Von.

I will never forget the shape Day'Von was in once we got him home. His underwear was stuck to his skin like glue because of the bowel movement that was pasted to his bottom. As I put water on his body, he screamed loudly. I knew then that he had experienced situations where he was not nurtured like he should have been.

I tried the more to get him cleaned up, so I soaked his body with wet towels. As I was cleaning his fragile body, I made a lifetime commitment. Though his two-year-old mind couldn't understand it fully, but I promised I would never let anything happen to him.

He was losing weight rapidly (7.5 lbs.), but I was determined to save him. I needed help, so I turned to a therapist. Once I made it to the therapist, she saw my desperate desire to have him well. I remember blatantly asking her, "How can I save this baby?"

She responded in a rather soothing tone, "That's easy, just love him!" Though I didn't believe I was capable of doing that, I was determined to give it my best effort. I read everything I could get my hands on. I went to the library and listened to constant tapes on how to be a mother.

Shhh...The Devil is Listening

I learned to say I love you with a smile.
I still wanted to connect with him more.

I saw myself in him. In fact, I really didn't envision his face. When I cared for him, I saw Pam. I saw me. I began to nurture him like I felt I should have been nurtured as a child.

Everything I always yearned for as a child I decided to pour into him. I treated him the best and gave him the best. Soon, I could tell the level of love that I exuded toward him was working for the good. He started gaining weight and started responding to the words 'I love you'. He no longer drank from the toilet as a measure of survival. He was on the road to becoming a very well nurtured baby. And for the first time in my life, I felt the love that healthily exuded from another person.

I became protective like he was my baby! I looked him into the eyes often and held close to my commitment "Ain't nothing every going to happen to you!"

My daughter started to come back around. This time she was pregnant with the next baby-Khloé. I watched how she cared for Day'Von so I opened my doors wholeheartedly to her. In the back of my mind, I still believed she was involved heavily in the drug scene. Soon, she started bringing drugs in my house. Knowing this, I began fighting for custody for the baby girl too.

Finally, once the baby girl, Khloé was 3 months old, I received custody for her as well. God blessed me twice with a baby.

Their mother turned to the streets again. When she came back the third time, my daughter still wasn't healthy, but she was pregnant again. I thought, "maybe God was going to bless with me with a third baby." Some babies might be rejected by many, but I made a commitment that they would be loved by me, no matter what! I knew that all babies, no matter the circumstances, were a blessing directly from God.

During my daughter's tumultuous season, I learned how to pray because of her. I knew she was in trouble, but I also knew she had been hurt. I saw the same pain in her that I had in me. Later she revealed that her mother's boyfriend would molest her when he was drunk. Immediately, I could identify with what I saw in her eyes. She also had a learning disability, like me. That made me love her even more and wanted to protect her.

I needed God to help me so that I could help them. I had

grown up in church but steered away. With everything going on, I went back to church.

The more I prayed; it seemed the worst things became. Drugs were still prominent, but at least she was in a state of mind that she wanted to come to my house to visit the children. However, she couldn't be left alone with them.

One Sunday afternoon she came over to the house. Originally, she was supposed to come two days prior, on Friday for family night. However, she called, "Can we do Saturday instead?" When Saturday arrived, she called and asked if we could move family night to Sunday. She kept wanting to change the day. I figured she probably wasn't going to show up Sunday, so finally I told her to come Monday on her regular visitation day.

That Sunday morning, I was getting ready to walk out the door to go to my church when the phone began to ring. My niece was on the other end of the phone line inviting me to her church for their friends and family day.
I decided to go. I pulled up in front of the church and my grandson Day'Von became really excited! He had visited the church before with his Pawpaw. While he was there, he would attend children's church. This time was different though. Children's church was canceled. Day'Von became so upset

because he didn't understand why it was closed. But before church got started in the main sanctuary, a group of ministers and deacons, all male, had formed a big circle around the sanctuary. They allowed the little boys to participate in the prayer circle as well. I remember one of the ministers pointed at Day'Von and invited him to come and join in prayer. Day'Von lit up like a Christmas tree as he stood in the prayer circle with all the men. After the men finished praying, Day'Von walked back to the pew where I was with the pride of George Jefferson (from the 80s show *The Jefferson's*). He looked up at me with this bright glow on his face and he said, "Guess what Nana. I got to pray with the big people!"

Once church ended, Day'Von was ecstatic to tell everyone about what happened during the service! From the store, to the restaurant, to the conversation inside the car, he expressed with glee how much this major opportunity made him proud!

Once we made it back home, I heard a knock on the door. To my surprise, it was my daughter. Her skin had cleared up and her belly was big and plump. It was extremely hot outside that day, so I hurriedly welcomed her inside.

The children were sleep. I watched her wake her babies up

from their naps. That day was a good day. I remember having a sense of great peace.

My daughter Jessica ran and played with the kids a lot that Sunday. My husband was in bed as he worked nights. I watched the children as they enjoyed their mom. They ate plenty of popsicles to keep themselves cool.

She came in the house, took the pillows off the couch and put them on the floor. They all laid there watching the movie *Happy Feet* for most of that evening.

As my daughter laid on the floor, I witnessed the baby's foot kicking through her stomach for the first time.

All of it was a miracle.
 The whole house was full of peace and love.

Soon it was time for bed. Khloé wasn't too cooperative that night. Instead of sleeping with her mom, she wanted to sleep with me. I put her in her bed, but she kept climbing out of her baby bed to come and sleep with me. I didn't fight it. She pulled herself up at the foot of the bed and crawled into my arms and went fast asleep.
Joy and peace were all in my house because all of my babies

were there under one roof.

We slept soundly for a few hours.

Then, suddenly I was woken up by a loud persistent noise. I got up quickly knocking over the bedside lamp. I didn't realize what I was hearing was our smoke alarm.

I rushed to where my daughter and grandson were sleeping. The door was shut, tightly. Beneath the door, I could see a red light beaming around. I could hear demonic sounds coming from behind the door as it rattled. It was all surreal.

I reached to push the door open. At the moment, my hand touched it, a big red ball of fire flew out. It was so large, it put a hole in my wall. I ran back to my room to grab Khloé. Smoke filled the space; I could barely see in front of me. I swayed my hand across my bed trying to locate Khloé's small body. I pulled her from the bed and immediately ran down the hallway holding on tightly to Khloé's belt. I held tightly to her belt as she dangled from my hands like a rag doll. She was wearing her belted denim *Hello Kitty* dress her mom purchased for her. The belt was the first thing I could grab, so I did. She wouldn't allow her mom to take her dress off before bed because she had become infatuated with how cute she looked earlier that day. Now, I was glad she kept it on.

By this time, my husband had already left for work. Several years before, I allowed a homeless gentleman to come and live in my home. Soon he became like a son to me. As I raced from the house, I screamed to him in the living room to get up because the house was on fire!

I opened the screened door as the fire rushed down the hallway towards us. Immediately I ran to my next-door neighbor, screaming, "My house is on fire, HELP!!!" She didn't answer. So, I stood in the middle of my front yard screaming with every bit of strength I had in my body, begging, pleading for somebody, anybody to help. My babies were still inside the house!

There was a lady that pulled up to my house in a Beatle Bug like car. The driver who heard me screaming in the neighborhood a few blocks over came over to see about me. Soon my neighbor Ms. Sally called the fire department. As they were en route, I wanted to help them myself. I pulled a small ladder from the side of my house. As I rested the ladder to the window, I saw that the bottom of the room floor where my grandson and daughter laid was engulfed in fire. I didn't see my daughter Jessica at all. I could see my grandson lying on the top bunk of the bunk beds. I shattered the window, but it was extremely hot. As I tried to climb in despite the heat, I heard an intense cracking noise as the bunk beds in which he laid fell in a large hole that had now encircled the room's floor.

I began to scream to the top of my lungs, calling on the name of Jesus. I begged God to help me save my babies. I remember my nephew running towards me screaming and he asked, "Aunt Pam, what's wrong?" I said, "The kids are in the house and Day'Von just fell in the fire!" A complete numbness came over me.

My mind began to realize what I was witnessing. I just couldn't believe my grandson; his mother and her unborn babies were engulfed in flames.

MY GOD PLEASE HELP!

The fire department seemed like they took their time to get to my place. Once they arrived, the water hose was too short to reach the hydrant to extinguish the fire, so they had to bring another truck with a longer fire hose.

It seemed as if my life was peering into a scene of a horror movie and everything seemed to be happening in slow motion.

Shhh...The Devil is Listening

I soon became incoherent.

The fire department entered what was left of my home. They extracted Jessica from the rubbish. She was sitting upright uncovered. Still holding to my hope. A bystander that knew me, screamed, "Pam, oh my God, look at her face!"

I thought she was alive. Once I looked back towards her, half of her face was gone. It was beyond surreal.

The policemen and firemen were all around walking away as they shook their heads in disbelief by the sight that they had witnessed.

I begged and pleaded for them to bring my grandson, Day'Von out to let me see him. Instead, they wanted me to go straight to the hospital. I begged him to let me wait, because I wanted to see Day'Von. He insisted that I get to the hospital at once.

In a sheer daze, I overheard family members and neighbors discussing various items. Some said, "I wonder if they had insurance." Others whispered, "I wonder if Jessica was high." Another one said, "I wonder if Day'Von was playing with matches or something." None of the accusations they made were true. They didn't even matter. I wanted my baby and I wanted him now!

Somehow, I made it to the hospital. The coroner came in and pronounced Jessica dead. At that moment it felt like someone had taken razor blades and put fire on the end of them and began ripping my heart apart. Then I screamed, "WHERE IS MY GRANDSON?" The detectives and coroner looking at me and then to one another and then they walked out the room. Never answering my question.

I needed answers and I needed them fast! However, no one would help whenever I asked about Day'Von.

As they exited the room, I noticed a petite black lady. I asked, "Will you do me a favor and find out where Day'Von is for me?" She didn't answer.

I laid in the hospital, and my room filled up with family and friends. My brother took wet washcloths and put them on my face. Still, every time I asked about Day'Von mostly everyone would leave the room. My brother's pastor and my pastor along with my brother stayed. It got to the point that the only thing I could hear was these three men saying, "Jesus, Jesus, Jesus!" I was in bad shape, but God blessed me with intercessors who were able to call on the Lord in my stead.

Shhh...The Devil is Listening

No one ever answered me regarding Day'Von. So, finally, I told them to get my daddy up there because he would tell me the truth. My dad was a very blunt man. However, one of them told me that my Daddy said he wasn't coming to the hospital. I thought, "When I needed him the most, he's not here for me." I was his only daughter. He should have been there!

I was filled with both rage and pain. My daddy should have been there for me!

In the midst of all of the chaos, there was a moment when I was in my room all alone. The little black lady showed up again. She kept walking back and forth in front of my door. She would gaze at me as if she knew me and wanted to tell me something. I began to feel myself being comforted in a way I had never experienced. When she walked by, I told her to come closer. She sat on the side of my bed. I asked if she could get my daddy to come. She said, "Don't be angry with your dad. He's standing in the gap for your baby. Your dad is at your house and said he was not leaving until all of Day'Von's bones were found." It was the first time I felt his love for me. Instantly a level of peace came over me.

I wanted to ask the little black lady that wore black framed glasses many more questions, but no one knew who I was talking about when I referenced her. I never saw her again. As

I processed the situation much later, I understand she was an angel. I believe my time with her was an angelic encounter God granted to bring me peace during the hell I was experiencing.

Nothing in that room survived that fire but two things: 1) a plastic angel statue that faced towards the bed that was badly burned and 2) my bible. They were smokeless and untouched.

During the conversation about my Dad staying at that house, I never internalized the fact, the "bones" meant Day'Von was also dead. He was gone. I never got a chance to say goodbye. That night though, all of them visited me in my dream. In the dream, Jessica was in a rocking chair holding the new baby. Day'Von was in an open field. He was carrying a flag. There was all white colors and clothes surrounding him. His purity of love shined through. Though I couldn't see the baby's face, I knew after the dream, that everything was alright with them. This provided some peace.

As I reflect, I was fortunate. I was able to nurture Day'Von for three years. It was a kind of relationship I had never experienced. Though he had only graduated preschool, he was the one who taught me how to love.

Shhh...The Devil is Listening

With the love and innocence of a five-year-old, he opened my heart in a way I had never experienced. He was my life. Hence, I was committed to making sure that nothing ever happened to Day'Von. With this fire, I let him down BIG TIME! He died on my watch. For a long time, the guilt that I held seemed unforgivable!

After all, I was just a stepmother and step-grandmother to my babies. I didn't feel worthy to feel the intense pain or love I felt. In reality, this was somebody's else family. At the point of their deaths, I held back my own tears and the expression of my own pain because I told myself, "There's no way you could be hurting like her biological parents are hurting." I was hurt, intensely. When the fire happened, I had never felt the level of pain that their deaths caused for me. This let me know that the level of love that I experienced was new and different.

Jessica was not a touchy-feely person either, but one day as I was cooking in the kitchen, she came in. She called my name, I responded, "What do you want?" She said, "Pam, I wish you would have been my Momma!" At the point, I knew exactly how she felt about me.

I believed God gave him, gave them, to me as gifts. I started to own how I felt about them. For the first time ever, I wept uncontrollably.

As the days passed, the constant thoughts of his body dropping into the pit of the fire disturbed me for days and years to come. Guilt tried to overtake me. It whispered and reminded me about my negligence. You see, each night I had established a routine of cleaning up each kid and praying over them before bed. Yet, the night before the fire I was entrenched with cleaning the house. I was busy preparing the linen for the guest room and washing and rehanging curtains. I was rather exhausted at the end of the night and forgot to pray over the children that night.

After the fire, I continuously blamed myself for the pain that the kids endured because I forgot to pray. Nevertheless, later on, God reminded me that Day'Von was covered because he got to pray with all of the men earlier in the prayer circle. This gave me a sense of relief. I was also relieved when we found out the cause of the fire. The fire was caused by a glitch in an extension cord that ran under the bed. Knowing that the cord caused the bed to catch fire and not because my daughter was doing something, she had no business, helped me on my journey to healing.

Shhh...The Devil is Listening

I became so absorbed in depression that I forgot about his sister, Khloé. She was two years old, the same age as Day'Von was when he first came to me. My emotional absence was not fair to her. Finally, after a year or so, I fought to snap out of the daze. I can remember it was like it was yesterday. She came in the room where I was twice, vying for my attention. I ignored it. The third time she came in, she told me she was hungry. Immediately, something in me shifted. It was at that point, I vowed to wholeheartedly take care of her. I renewed my commitment to ensure that everything about her would be safe. I invested all that I had to give and sought help when needed because she deserved it.

I enrolled her in school. She went to the same school Day'Von attended. As I took her inside one day (at this point it was nearly three years after Day'Von's passing) the school officials gave me all of Day'Von's schoolwork and projects. In the packet there were a lot of his paintings and drawings and other school activities he had completed. There was also a video included in the package. I held on to the video for some time until I mustered up enough courage to open it. I popped it into the video cassette recorder. The video consisted of different recordings of different events that he was involved in at school. He was so full of pride that day. We were so proud of his growth and accomplishment. He had come a long way from the neglected baby in the parking lot.

I watched the video intently. At the end of the video, Day'Von was climbing the steps to get on his school bus, then he turned around and looked at the camera and waved. He said the words that I had longed to hear, "Goodbye Nana!"

My baby had told me goodbye after all! This made way for my healing journey to begin.

I needed to live. Khloé deserved me.

However, as I pushed to live, I first had to face some demons.

Ironically, after watching my babies burn in that fire it was as if God had ignited a fire within me. He wouldn't allow me to suppress this level of deep hurt ever again. It was as if the demons that were suppressed for decades were freed from their cages. So, though terribly tragic, the fire kindled a desire in me to open the vault of my own childhood wounds.

3

THE FAMILY

When I consider the fullness of my life, I think of the biblical story of Job. Job was a man God trusted to endure some of the most intense pains of life. Within its 42 chapters, Job goes from being an innocent person that quickly transformed into a figure that represented turmoil and grief. Nevertheless, his life ends representing a man of great stature and wealth.

Although I couldn't read much as a child, there is one bible story that I remembered, it was about the life of Job. Job was called perfect and upright. Nonetheless, within the first twenty verses, Job lost his children, his sheep, and fire consumed his servants and camels. His oxen and asses were all slain. Of all that Job loss that day, I'm certain the loss of his children grieved him greatly. Every child, just like Day'Von and Khloè, are gifts from the Lord.

Job experienced hell on earth. In many ways, I felt I was Job. During Job's story, his friends turned their back on him. His wife suggested that he simply curse God and die. Much of my journey I felt as if I were dead. At certain points in my life, I was numb to the reality and intensity of what had happened to me.

My childhood did not represent the joy that gifts usually bear. However, I was lucky to be gifted with two grandmothers. My mother's mother was a dark skin rough woman. She was a fighter. She was a no-nonsense very blunt, yet a giving woman. You never had to guess what she was thinking, because she was quick to tell you whether you actually wanted to hear it or not. Every obstacle that she was confronted with, she took head on with her pistol in tow.

On the other hand, my dad's mom was a bit gentler. I loved her a lot, but for many years I viewed her as a 'weak' woman because I witnessed her cry a lot. The same people that caused her grief, were the same ones she blessed. At first, this made no sense to me. Eventually, it all came together for me. She was a God-fearing lady who truly believed in the God she served. Instead of using a gun, she 'fought' with God as her guide. I was her "Pammy." I could do no wrong in her sight. She adored me and I loved her endlessly. She taught me much about her Savior through the life that she led. I remember her specifically teaching me how to call on the name of Jesus. I never realized how soon I would need him. In fact, at five, when I was molested by our friendly neighbor, I would have to call on Jesus a lot.

Before I go into detail about that, I want to give you a full glimpse of my childhood. I would like to think that my family was pretty normal. I had both my biological parents in our home. One older brother that was 3 years my senior. This made him a bit overprotective of me. I expected that because it was normal for siblings during that time. My brother Eric and I would fight quite often. I would call him 'blackie' or 'jew' baby and then I would stick my tongue out at him and take off running. He was much darker than me; I was a pretty fair skinned child. Often, he would retaliate by calling me a 'high yellow white girl' and throw a handful of rocks at me. Regardless of our childhood spats, I knew my brother loved me.

Sometimes our family would travel together during the summer months. All the other time, mom and dad worked frequently. Mom sustained a neck and back injury at the plant where she worked as a machine operator. She was also a seamstress and worked outside of the house. My dad was a maintenance man at an apartment complex. He also earned income from many other jobs like painting and doing electrical work. Dad was a licensed electrician. Besides family, what dad loved the most was his horses. If he wasn't working, you could find dad at the fairgrounds getting his horses ready for a race.

He was a Vietnam veteran and because of it, was a well-disciplined man. I learned a lot from my parents. My knack for design came from mom and I learned to paint and inherited great attention for detail from my dad. If someone ever tried to mess with his family, you would see another side of my dad. He would kill without a second thought.

During the early 1970s our neighborhood was pretty close knit and safe. I remember my parents loving to entertain family and friends in the backyard where they had a brand-new shed built for shelter, when it rained. They both loved playing a good game of Pokeno[1], Spades, or Dad's favorite card game *Tank*.

---

[1] This was a classic bingo-style games that combined poker and keno.

Shhh...The Devil is Listening

As I reminisce about some sweltering summer nights, I realize we never owned an air conditioner. To keep things cool, my parents would keep a full-size fan bolted to the front windows. When the fan wasn't enough, they would keep the front door wide open throughout the entire night as we slept.

Eric was highly involved in various sports teams and when I wasn't participating in my local Girls Scout program, I was left at home with some of our neighbors.

To the direct right of us, were my babysitters' house. They were a nice couple. They didn't have any children and they adored me. At least it started that way. I liked them a lot. They even took me fishing a few times. I remember working puzzles together with the couple. Unlike my own family, they really took an interest in me. Nevertheless, things shifted quickly. When my parents were around, the wife would squeeze my cheeks and rant and rave about how much she "loved" me. Just as soon as they left, she would cuss me out. One night, I just walked into the room she was in and she yelled, "Sit your fat ass down somewhere! I can't stand you!" Things were taking a turn for the worse. I would go over a few times a week. One particular time, my dad forgot to pay them. Trust me, they took it out on me! The woman became extremely angry. She said, "The motherfucker is supposed to have all this money and he didn't even pay me! I'm not watching her fat ass!" She continued, "Take that little bitch home and leave her there!" Our house was right next door to their home. Little did I know; my life was getting ready to change forever.

The neighbor to the left, two doors down, drove a fancy car. He was very well-dressed, light-complexioned with hazel colored eyes and he had what some would call "good"[2] hair. He was also an ex-military man and a typical "pretty" boy type. He could have gotten any woman he wanted, yet he chose me, the 5-year-old neighbor's kid instead. He was a good friend of my dad. Dad trusted him. However, this neighbor became my molester.

He watched us closely. Growing up Eric and I were pretty close, but things changed when the beatings and the molestation started. I knew Eric loved me but soon my own love for people would be beat out of me. The neighbor watched us all. He noticed that Eric and I didn't bond as much anymore. He noticed that my brother was a bit more favored by my parents than me. He played on it all.

---

[2] "Good" hair is the usually the resulting hair texture of mixed raced children. It is characterized with fine strands and a wavy texture. "Bad" hair was the hair that was typically textured and coarse in feel.

Shhh...The Devil is Listening

It started by gaining my trust. He was very nice. He even gave me gifts. He originally lured me in by giving me candy. He kept me supplied with lots of candy. The candy was the bait to lure children in. I would share the candy with all the different kids in the neighborhood. He would want me to report to him who I shared the candy with. His plan was to go ask them to give the candy back to him. If the kids didn't have the candy, they would be under his control. So, I didn't tell.

During my visits to come get more candy, my molester soon convinced me that my family didn't love me, and anger arose within me. This led to him touching me in between my legs and eventually he put his hands inside my panties. He never fondled where it felt good. It was always rough and extremely intense. It started with his hands in my vagina and then his fully erected penis. He threatened me not to tell a soul!

I would go to school and interact with other kids and they would want some of the candy he gave me. In my 5-year-old mind, I thought sharing the candy with them would make him molest them too. In my effort to protect them, I told them no! My 'no's' backfired on me swiftly! Many of the kids and even their parents called me mean. Instantly, I became known as the mean girl. None of the kids liked me and their parents hated me. They never invited me to any of their children's birthday parties, let alone step foot on their front lawns. I became isolated and began to withdraw all the more. However, I knew if they ate the candy, he was going to do to them what he did to me. Sometimes, I wished I would have shared the candy because I know their lives would have been changed forever just like mine.

Candy wasn't the end of his gifts. One of the next gifts he gave me was a $1 bill and a doll wrapped in a nice box. At one point, I felt really special! However, swiftly that feeling changed. One day when he got angry with me, he said, "Give me my doll back, give me my $1 back!" I went in the house and tried my best to make the doll pretty by combing her hair and fixing up her clothes. Yet, when I tried to give it back to him, my primping was never enough. He said, "Well, where is the box it came in?" Terrified, I stood there without words, because I knew my mom had thrown the box in the trash weeks earlier. Next, he asked for the $1 bill back. I was excited to get that because $1 was pretty easy to come by. When I saw him again, I tried to give him $1, but he wouldn't accept it because it wasn't the *exact* $1 bill that he had given me. Once I got a bit older, I learned that these were all mental games he was playing on me. Our involvement didn't end there though, things began to escalate.

Shhh...The Devil is Listening

Once, while my dad was away, I was in the back playing with some of his paint brushes. One of the brushes broke. My dad discovered it and was upset, that he vented to my molester about what I did. The molester would later use this to threaten me and put a larger wedge between me and my parents. When the molester gave me my first beating, he said that he owed me this beating because my dad told him to beat me because of the damage done to the paint brushes.

He often felt he had to teach me a lesson and this time it was a lesson in love. He filled a long knee length sock with a full deck of cards and asked if I loved my parents. I responded, "Yes!" He swung and hit me over my back with the loaded socks continuously... it wasn't until I said "no" did the beatings cease. He was grooming me to be "his" and "his" only.

He started to beat his dog in the open yard to show me what would happen if I ever told anyone that I was his newly found obsession. I never murmured a word. In fact, he stuffed my mouth with socks to be sure that my silence remained.

Another time he nearly suffocated me by putting a sock, what felt like down my throat and a pillow on my face. I had to turn my face to the side so I would maintain my breath. He wanted to ensure no would hear the echoes from the intensity of the pain I was getting ready to experience. He pulled off my pants and ripped down my panties. Laying naked, I couldn't see but I could hear the flickering of the cigarette lighter as he pinned me down. I began to feel some warmth from the heat near my vagina. I didn't know what was happening. He held my legs with his and the burning flames from the cigarettes lit directly on my vagina. I screamed as loud as I could! During each scream, he increased his body weight of the pillow to lessen the shrills while yelling names like, "Shut up fat bitch, quiet you whore!"

I just knew someone would bust threw the doors immediately, but no one responded. There was blood everywhere!

I laid there in shock. I can remember gently putting my hand between my legs where I could feel these bubble-like things forming on my vagina. I was in so much pain that my entire body was shaking. Though, I could no longer feel my legs, I could see that they wouldn't stop shaking. Somehow, I took my hand that I used to feel my vagina, to wipe tears from my face. There was blood on my hands that somehow ended up in my mouth. It was if someone had glued my mouth shut because I could no longer open it. The blood had died up and sealed my lips shut. I'm not certain how long I laid there in the bed filled with blood. I remember competing voices in my mind. It was if my grandmothers were in the room with me. I could hear their voices. One was saying, "You better fight and I mean it!" The other would say, "Pammy baby, say Jesus, call him baby, say Jesus." Then, I remember fearing my mother. I had wet the bed and mother always told me that big girls never wet the bed.

Somehow the babysitting couple made it over to view the scene. There was blood everywhere. They tore me from the bed and put me in the bathtub to help him clean up the evidence of the crime that had been committed against me. Instead of turning on the water, they brought in towels and buckets of bleach. They started pouring bleach over my fragile body as blood slipped down the drain.

I knew I would die that day. I wondered all that while, what had I done to deserve such treatment. ***I was silently being murdered and felt complete abandonment.***

My mind and emotions started to slip away in order to survive the abuse.

My room was in the back of the house. The fan kept us cool and took up the entire length and width of the window. If lights were on in my room, anyone on the outside could see directly inside. I hated that fan!

At night, when my molester was drunk during the

summertime, he would come and put his face near the window fan. He would make scary noises all while whispering threats about cutting my head off and come on the inside to get me.

If my molester wasn't tormenting me in the fan, my sitters would come and do the same. I had a secret of theirs. The secret was that they didn't babysit me and keep me safe like they had promised my parents. In fact, I remember a conversation that the neighbors had with my molester. They said, "If he(referring to my dad) finds out about this, he's going to kill us all!" My dad was known as the crazy military man on the block. So, it was important for them to continually torment through the fan because this would keep me scared and would continue to keep me silent.

I was stuck! I had to do something and fast.

I started relying on saving myself as best I could. Naturally like most toddlers and children I slept on my stomach, but as the abuse persisted, I trained myself to sleep on my back. I figured if I slept on my stomach and my back was to the door, I never would see him coming. When I slept on my stomach, it was an easy point of access for him. As I grew older and learned to sleep on my stomach, it became a protective mechanism against my molester.

Being molested, I had to develop some type of internal survival mechanism to help me cope. Otherwise, I would have taken my own life. I remember I would go home from school some days and pass the local park and see kids on the swings laughing. I often wondered what was so funny. During the molestation, my laughter, my joy, and my innocence was stolen from me. I never wanted to wear a little dress when I was a child. Many people around me thought it was weird. Yet, as a 7-year-old I was forced to consider survival strategies. I wanted to wear pants instead, that way, it would take my molester a long time to get to me. With a dress, he could just pull it up and there was the prize. I wanted to make him work.

Over the next few days, I could barely walk. Green, red and yellow pus protruded from my body. I put my hand down there to comfort it as times. Once, just after bringing comfort to the fire that was my vagina, I touched my mouth. The taste of blood never left me.

I began to withdraw even further. In school, I was in the learning-disabled classes. Our classes were held in the trailers that resembled a jail. It had steel paneling and everything around us was dull. The floors were cement and no light shined inside our classroom. It felt like a prison.

Every time I walked past one of the teachers, it was like a voice inside of me screamed "HELP, HELP!!!" I was hoping some of the teachers would have caught on to what was happening. They never did. I started to hate the teachers. They called me stupid and retarded. I even had a teacher tell me I needed to be put in a nut house because I wouldn't talk. I spent most of my school days in the corner because of my tiredness. The teachers would catch me sleeping in class. Hence, standing up would be my punishment in an effort to keep me awake. I was punished for being a victim, but I didn't commit a crime. However, I learned how to sleep while standing in the corner. I hated all of my teachers.

My teachers would also get on me about taking too long but each time I used the restroom it was a traumatic experience. Imagine what it felt like having to peel my panties that were melted into the soon to be scabs from the cigarette burn with pus protruding, in order to urinate after lunch. Every time I pulled down my panties, I tried my best to not peel off a newly formed scab. Nine times out of ten, that was unsuccessful.

At church, things weren't much different. One day, at our Methodist Church, I was moving and squirming on the church bench. One of the trustees came over and pulled me by my arms and shouted, "I said to be still!" At which point, he smashed me back down to my seat by my shoulders. I was only moving because of the burns on my vagina had become inflamed. I started to scream and just went outside of the sanctuary to the front of the church. Once I made it outside, my molester was outside fraternizing with the neighbors that lived across the street from the church. It was like I could never escape him, no matter where I went. I was scared and confused. I had to be silent because I believe he planned to kill me eventually.

I had only come that night because I thought I would be protected in the sanctuary. They sent me back outside. I was scared, I was confused, and I had to be silent.

By the time I made it to middle school, I quickly realized I wasn't a virgin anymore. I hesitated into relationships because I knew I didn't have a virginity to give. So, I played along in conversations with friends, trying my best to appear as if I still had my innocence.

The older and bigger I got, the more aggressive the abuse became.

I was tall for a middle schooler. Soon, I outgrew him in height. I was even taller than my dad. I started to look and dress weird because most of my pants were too short because of my height. In fact, the kids called my pants "high water."

I learned to depend on me well before I learned to depend on God. I needed to get stronger. So, I started playing football around 11 or 12 years old. The boys didn't welcome me on the field, but I would taunt them and call them all sorts of names. I called them "sissy this and this sissy that!" So, naturally they wanted to rough me up. They didn't show me any mercy. That is exactly what I wanted. It was exactly what I needed. They played with me like I was a boy. Little did they know that this was strength training for my abuse.

My molester would throw me on the ground and tackle me. The more I played football, the more I was prepared to handle the physical nature of the abuse. By this time, I no longer showed any emotion. I no longer gave him a response. This made him even more angry. During the time he was forcibly having sex with me, I was able to go to a place in my mind to fight the abuse. My body was there but I traveled to another location in my mind and emotions.

At the age of 13, I experienced my breaking point.

During that time, I had a little dog named Coco. Coco was my best and only friend. She was there the night I sustained all my burns and she even watched as my soul was murdered. Every horrific thing that ever happened to me, Coco was there. I refused everything he commanded me to do. I had gotten to where I couldn't feel pain anymore and he couldn't do anything else to me because I was officially broken. So, I would respond

Shhh...The Devil is Listening

to him with the words, "Go to hell!" I was taller than he was at that point and stronger than an ox from playing football. So, I was ready for him! One day, he saw my dog and grabbed her and started beating on her. Coco was small and fragile. Then he started choking the dog. I could hear Coco struggling to breathe. Finally, I begin to beg him to save her. Then the unthinkable happened.

He made me get on my knees and perform oral sex on him, while calling him "Daddy" and told me to tell him it was good. After I was done, he masturbated all over my face. Afterwards he hacked and spit in my face and told me I was nothing but trash! This was my breaking point. I agreed with the acts in order to save my dog. Though, no one ever tried to save me.

I cried, but at 13, that was my last and final cry.

To this day, when I'm engaging sexually, I have a difficult time as this often causes triggers of the encounter I had as a 13-year-old. There is a rage on the inside of me that I can't hide. Often times, I will have to leave.

There's a loss in my memory from ages 13-16 years old. Since that encounter, I have a difficult time reliving and remembering what happened in my life from ages 13-16. My pastor tells me that my brain couldn't take anymore, so as a protective mechanism, it shut itself down. I tried to regain memories and experiences during those years but cannot.

When I got off my knees, I became a beast. I became belligerent. I didn't respect anybody else. I started stealing. I started smoking cigarettes. Back then, they didn't ask for identification at the liquor store. I would go up there and say I came for a neighbor and they would give me the liquor of my choice. They trusted kids to do the right thing. I was lying, cheating and stealing. I needed to numb the pain. I remember drinking my grandmother's peppermint snap, and other cough medicines. I took in anything I could get my hands on. I even had cigars. It provided a buzz that I felt I needed.

We came up in a time that we had to respect our elders. By this time, I refused to say any of this anymore. They didn't like me. They had given me the mean title and finally I started living up to that title-"MEAN, She ain't shit! She's going have a whole bunch of kids, look at her! She'll never amount to anything!"

This thing was getting the best of me. I remember getting to a point of complete outrage. I didn't feel love from many people. I started to wonder why my parents didn't notice my limp. I wondered why I felt so alone and unloved.

Shhh...The Devil is Listening

Yet, I knew Eric loved me, because he would take up for me when his friends would try to convince the other kids that I didn't draw one of the pictures that I had sketched. I overheard him trying to convince them that they were wrong, and I was gifted. These memories represented his love for me, yet, I still remember that during that time I began to change inside. My way of thinking about my immediate family started to totally shift. It was like the molester had helped me create this evilness towards them and a rage began to erupt inside of me. So much so, that I started to experience this sound of screaming inside my head. It got intense. I can't pinpoint exactly when, but it was between the ages of 11-13, one night I took my head and started to bust out all the windows in our home. As I banged my head to the windows the screams rang louder in my head. I could hear laughter from my family in the background. They yelled all sorts of names toward me, "crazy, stupid, insane..." I had hoped to knock my brains out to silence the screams. My family was convinced I was on drugs, but I just wanted the screams to stop.

Hate began to fester in my heart deeply.

Somehow, the screaming started to cease, but my anger towards my family only intensified. The older I got the more I started to notice that there were things about me that were different.

In high school, because I had started to notice the pattern of my molester using my parents' words against me, I didn't share much. I was being silenced. My friends were talking about what teenagers talked about like birth control and safe sex. In my mind, I was already a whore because I had had sex and was not married. Nothing about the sex I experienced was "safe". So, I persisted with this secret and stayed silent about that too. I was convinced that I had nothing of value to give in a relationship at the intimate level.

I was not going to get married. I was destined to become an "old maid." Though, I had a learning disability, I still wrote a letter to God. I decorated it perfectly. I remember drawing flowers over the top of the letter I's. I needed help. It was a weight all too much to bear, alone. Something needed to change, and fast!

Home life was horrible! Every time my parents would come home, they would find something I did that was "wrong.". Anger festered within me. I could have easily murdered them and not have one stitch of remorse. Many of their words killed me on the inside. They told me that I'd never amount to anything. On the other hand, they were always ecstatic about how successful my brother would be in sports. It was difficult to digest this grave level of difference in the love they displayed towards us.

They were the sweetest loving people in public. However, behind closed doors, things would be different, at least towards me. I was overweight. They often complained about my weight. I was called "big fat bitch, big fat" that. I felt like I was never enough for them.

As a result, I devised a grand plan. It would all go down on my 16th birthday.

Granted, by this time, I had become the typical teenager from hell. I had built the mentality of, "nobody is going to make me cry anymore! They will cry and suffer before I do." I was done with hurting at the hands of anybody, including my family. When I cried, I was called a crybaby. I was told, "Go and sit down somewhere." When I smiled, the molester would ask, "What are you smiling for? Nothing's that funny!" So, I quickly turned that smile into a frown. And I would get criticized there. Other parents would say, "Why don't you ever smile? What's wrong with you? Your face is really tore up? " So, I didn't have nowhere to go. I began to feel like a puppet. This made the angry fester eternally on the inside of me.

I knew where my dad kept his gun in the house.

I was so happy for my birthday that year. I cooked a big birthday dinner for myself. However, the celebration was that I was getting set to take them out of my life. ***I didn't care about going to prison because I was already in jail.*** I had no fear of any of that. To me, prison would become my escape route. I figured, if I killed them, I wouldn't have to hear them nag me all the time and report to my molester the things that I had done. I figured, if I went to jail, I would get away from my molester. It was a win-win situation!

I have been a hustler since as early as I could remember. When I was a kid, I would rake leaves for the elderly during the fall and shovel snow during the winter months. I had several clients. Every time they gave me money, I would run to put my money in my *Miracle Whip* jar. I kept the jars in the back of my dad's shed in the gutter. No one else knew about it.

On my 16th birthday, on the day I had planned to murder all of them, I walked to the local Piggly Wiggly and stole food to prepare from them. I prepared everybody their favorite foods. I remember that was one of the happiest days of my life.

Whatever my family said about me, they didn't care about who they said it in front of. There was an evident hate that they had

Shhh...The Devil is Listening

developed for me. While my brother and I were typical teenagers, we still argued, fussed and fight. There were many fights where my parents believed him over me. It was apparent, that he was their favorite.

So, I wanted to take something from them that they loved. My dad played with his guns. He would take the bullets out and put them back in. I learned how to do it too. Watching him, I learned how to unlock the safety clip. That night, I got the gun from my dad's room and put it in the wood burning stove we had in the living room. I left a bit of the handle out so I could grab it quickly. I was happy that day because I knew that I was getting ready to hurt them, by killing my brother. I was going to kill him, and they were going to watch. Next, I would kill both of them. Then, I would be finally free once they were all dead.

I didn't know much about the Holy Spirit then. I went into the bathroom, but it was like something went in there before me. There was a folded newspaper laying on the small table right in front of the toilet. As I sat down, I noticed an advertisement at the top of the page. It had a phone number next to it that stuck out like a sore thumb. I called the number and a very soft-spoken lady answered. We spoke and she said, "Well the cost is $210 per month. If you want to see the place, I'm down here right now." I hung up the phone and got on my 10-speed bicycle to see the lady at her place about 15 minutes from where I lived.

Hurriedly, I left all of my festivities, and rode down the street in excitement. There was a little frail old lady waiting. I told her I wanted the place. She never asked me my age. She never asked me about my parents. Nothing. She just told me the rent amount. I told her I would take it. She let me know that she would leave all the utilities on so I would not have to pay a deposit. I left her immediately to go and get the money that was at my shed. I moved out that day. I had saved up enough money that I didn't have to pay rent for at least four months. I had money to purchase other necessities.

On the ride back to garner my savings, I thought: "I'll never have to return to this god forsaken house again because I never wanted to see any of them again." My feelings towards them was past any kind of hate that you could ever image.

That day ended with me riding my bicycle back and forth moving my stuff into my new apartment. Those first few nights, I remember laying on the floor of my apartment with no blankets or pillows. However, for the first time in my life I had a true sense of peace. With that peace, I was able to use

Shhh...The Devil is Listening

one of the trash bags filled with clothes as a makeshift pillow that night. My blanket was one of my oversized coats. Even though I didn't truly know God, God showed himself to me that day. I didn't kill my family, so my path was rerouted.

I couldn't really see how He worked everything out to get me out of that house. After I moved out of my parent's house, I didn't think about killing anymore. The negativity being around my family had taken its final toll on me. I vowed to myself that I would be homeless before I went back to that hell hole.

They say, be careful what you ask for because you might just get it. I remember, when times really got rough at my house, I left. I made up in my mind that the streets were better than my hell hole of a home. This was one of the hardest choices I've made. I was broken, in fact, this was an understatement. I had become convinced, by my molester, that my parents didn't love me. I had lost my ability to pray or even call on the name of Jesus. The pain had won! I no longer believed God loved me. I saw myself as if I was born into a black pit. In this pit, there was no love, no laughter. Everything was dark. Many days I didn't know whether or not I was still alive. My hope was gone. I felt like I was born into hell. I asked God why he didn't love me and what had I done wrong. I would just hear silence. I would then beg him to take my life. I still had a bedroom in my parents' home, but it felt like a torture chamber. I felt safer sleeping in abandoned cars or under wooden bleachers at the park. As dangerous as it may have seemed, I felt safe being away from the house I grew up in.

I felt alone. I was on my own. I learned to survive. It was very difficult, at first, but running saved my life. My sole mission was survival. I never worried about food or clothes. I was more concerned about my mind. The bible says you only need the faith the size of a mustard seed, but at that point, I didn't have that. All I had was hatred and pain. I was a ticking time bomb. People didn't bother me because I never smiled. I didn't have to answer many questions because I looked pretty mean. I didn't trust anyone and sometimes couldn't trust myself.

Even today, when I consider the things I endured, some would say that I should be ashamed of myself. My response would be: "try carrying my cross before you judge."

I chose to become homeless to just have a little piece of freedom, even though I didn't understand fully what it all meant.

4

THE FIGHT

Shortly after leaving my parents' house, I found a job at Piggly Wiggly. I worked in the bakery decorating wedding and birthday cakes. I enjoyed it thoroughly. However, I was only making $3.35 per hour, which was minimum wage at the time. Plus, because I was still in high school, I was only allowed minimal hours. Consequently, I didn't have money to pay my bills. Money got tight really quick, but I knew going back home was not an option! I had to turn the volume up of my life. So, I turned to the streets. I was desperate to make that money so I wouldn't end up back home.

The level of love I needed because of the abuse I endured was not available in my home, so I turned to the streets. I got desperate. You name it, I did it! But I didn't know anything about the streets! I was what they called GREEN.

First, I needed to learn quickly how to make ends meet. Starting out, I didn't have people to teach me the ropes, so I learned as I went. I would steal clothes from Woolworth and even the Salvation Army. There weren't any $1 stores. I remember the more advanced thieves would make fun of me because I was stealing from the Salvation Army. They'd say, "Green, she Green." I had been through hell and highwater, so I challenged them to teach me or shut the hell up in making fun of me! Soon, they began to teach me, and they taught me well.

I had to learn to fight quickly. When you're in the streets there are two things you must learn to survive. First, if you're in the streets, either you are going to live or die so you better learn to fight. And secondly, either you are going to choose jail or stay free. In order to stay free, you cannot be caught. These are the Rules of the Streets.

I never worried about dying because I was already dead. I was cutting with knives and razor blades. I was beating folks in the streets with baseball bats, woodchucks, hammers, you name it! It was what I used to survive.

My first friend was a 16-year-old girl who had recently given birth to her third child. She had become a pro at stealing to take care of her children. She helped me become more advanced so I could achieve my goal of never going back to my parents' home. One night she and I got into a fight with some other people from out of town at the club. During the fight, she got hurt pretty badly. There was blood everywhere! However, she had a warrant out for her arrest, so she didn't want to go to the hospital. Instead, some of the people from the club took her to a local house. At the local house, it was this woman who was known as a "house doctor." She was known to help younger women from the streets. This lady was Effie May. Even though my home girl lost her sight in one of her eyes, Effie May helped stitch her up that night. Effie May wasn't a beautiful woman. She had many battle wounds on her face like she also had to fight her way through life to survive. However, what made her beautiful despite all her scars, was her compassion. She was a soft-spoken woman. As many times as I messed up, she never judged me. In fact, she encouraged me with her show of love, compassion, forgiveness and guidance. She was a prayer warrior, and most importantly she displayed peace and joy.

Following that night, I formed an unbreakable bond with the women at the house. The bond was so strong, I considered them my street sisters. The house was a place for prostitutes. I was still underage and never got into prostituting, but they did teach me how to process and sell cocaine. They had clients selling their bodies and I had my clients who purchased my dope. I didn't ask them any questions about their lives and they never asked me anything about mines. (Street knowledge suggests that you mind your business before you are killed.) My sisters taught me a lot like how to put my make up on and how to dress like a respectful woman. I felt so safe when I was around my sisters; it was 48 of them. Even though it may have been a prostitute house, I never heard anyone getting put down or called out of their names. It felt like home to me. I knew they loved me and wanted the best for me. This was the first time I ever truly experienced this type of love and care. I never cared what others thought of me staying with them. Frankly, I didn't give a DAMN about people's opinions about me hanging out with these women. I saw them as my sisters and my family. With me having that many sisters, I was able to try all different kinds of drugs. I attempted crack cocaine, powder coke, marijuana too. I didn't like any of it! However, I did sale $1 or $2 joints (marijuana) sometimes, to make easy change. Then someone from the house let me try heroin. With heroin,

Shhh...The Devil is Listening

I was able to sleep and get the kind of high I was looking forward to enjoying. I needed to get some sense of peace from all the hell that I experienced.

By this time, I was being courted by guys to be in a relationship. It was difficult to engage sexually for a sense of pleasure because of the war I had lived through. In order to not stick out too much like a sore thumb or a weirdo, I engaged sexually. However, I had to numb myself with drugs in order to remind myself that I was with my partner instead of my molester.
At times, things started to feel like they were getting better. There were a few things I still remained silent about in my life though.

With the life I lived, you had to keep moving no matter what. If you stopped, there was a chance you could fall apart. Even though my street sisters and Ms. Effie said they loved me, it just wasn't enough for me. I walked around with a secret. My secret was I had a lot of hate and anger festering on the inside of me. I needed to go where I could really fit in. Being around upbeat spirits was making me feel worse. My spirit had been murdered and no one seemed to understand what that meant. So, I started to hang with a group of people that were more ruthless than me. Like me, they didn't know that smiles existed. I remember them asking me where I was from. I said, "from the belly of the beast. I have no family because I am dead." Then they asked if I wanted to join the family, because they were also dead. They explained what had to take place. After explaining the process, I said, "Let's get it on!" I wasn't scared because I was already dead.

Although, being severely beaten while naked for the initiation process of the gang was difficult for some, it was nothing for me. I had already experienced the worse as a child. The difficult part, however; was the embarrassment of my gang sisters seeing those cigarette scars. They saw them once I got dressed after the initiation process. Still, for a long time I wouldn't say anything even though I knew they saw them.

I remember all my gang family welcoming me into the family. I recall meeting my General and his words were, "In this house we show love. No Love, No Loyalty. You Show Love, You Get Loyalty." He continued, "Welcome to hell where we will take care of you now!" It may have been hell for the ones who have never experienced hell, but for me, I had found where I needed to be. I fit in there. I found my home. It was very easy for me to show my loyalty to the family. Still, I didn't give a damn about anyone or anything. It didn't bother me to hear someone beg and plead for life. I loved that life because I could take my hatred out on people who had no regard for life, just

Shhh...The Devil is Listening

like me. I had no feelings and no remorse. My mantra was, "kill or be killed.' Who was I? I was Punknella[3], one of Satan's kids. If you bothered us, we were coming for you with no mercy. Soon, I found that even all the hateful acts didn't make me happier. I was in the pit of hell, where you can't get out freely.

The streets were like a mirror for me. I had to grow up and face the somber music of what my life had become.

It was a street house, but for me with was a safe house. I felt safe there. I never witnessed them lay down with all the men. So, I maintained my respect for them even though I knew what they were doing when I wasn't around. It was as if they shielded me from all of the horrors. Effie May treated me better than my own mother. Effie May became family. She became street mom.

I became a professional stealer. I knew the timing of the camera systems. I knew when it would turn in my direction. I knew how it all worked. I could go inside the store empty handed and could come out with the entire store inside my bag. I would rehearse stealing like average high schoolers would practice their band instruments or algebra problems.

---

[3] My gang family called me Punknella (meaning ruthless). The name, however, came from my auntie. She said I resembled a little round pumpkin face when I was a baby. My street sisters from the safe house called me Pamella (meaning laid back).

The streets became my family.

I never went back home. I hoped they never made me come back. I threatened them. I remember telling my parents, "if you made me come back to your house, I would make your life a living hell!" I was serious. They never did bother me.

I became a true demon. I started to wear black clothing and black lipstick and all black make-up. I died my hair jet black. I was gone! I was cold. It was like I had no feeling. It was like I didn't have a soul. Nothing. I had no remorse. By this time, I couldn't even cry.

On the other hand, I felt horrible because I wanted to feel normal. I wanted to cry when my friends were giving birth. I couldn't. I didn't know how to cry when I saw someone accomplish something major like graduation. In fact, I often wondered what it felt like to cry happy tears. It was a mystery to me. I didn't understand that. I didn't know what it felt like to receive or give a sincere hug. **It was like I had transformed into something unreal in order to survive.**

Because of abandonment issues, I wouldn't allow anyone to get close or let my guard around my heart down. Love and care had abandoned me. I didn't know how to let my guard down because I had become so use to fighting.

When I was soft and gentle, no one wanted to hear me. When I became hardened by life, it was as if everyone wanted to listen then. By that time, I was done talking. I was only swinging and fighting and flipping over tables.

Eventually, I met a group of friends that had known the streets much better than I did. The more we spent time, the more I learned the ropes. I learned how to steal to get more money and lots of things. I learned how to fight. I got into lots of fights while in the streets and had multiple run ins with the police.

I started stealing all sorts of items in order to get money. However, I wasn't that good at it yet though. Then I was selling crack cocaine. I learned to process it and make it into a rock instead of powder.[4] The powder could be sold for $10 per bag, but the rock version would sell for $30. Then I learned how to REALLY start stealing. We moved from stealing at *Woolworth* to stealing

---

[4] [4]Cocaine is a hydrochloride salt in its powdered form, while crack cocaine is derived from powdered cocaine by combining it with water and another substance, usually baking soda (sodium bicarbonate). After cocaine and baking soda are combined, the mixture is boiled, and a solid forms. Once it's cooled and broken into smaller pieces, these pieces are sold as crack. Retrieved from https://americanaddictioncenters.org/cocaine-treatment/differences-with-crack.

$3000-$4000 leather jackets. Gangbanging, stealing, and selling drugs. ***I wasn't worried about going to jail, I was already in prison. I wasn't worried about dying because I was already dead.*** I died a long time ago and I didn't see anybody crying. So, when I saw people cry after a death, I didn't understand.

School became a thing of the past. They passed me along, not because I was proficient in all of the work, but because they didn't want to be *bothered* with me.

The street way accepted me, yet I grew even colder.
I didn't care about nothing and nobody!

Despite everything though, somehow, I knew I was going to make it.

Somehow, I never let myself really get comfortable. Deep down I knew I didn't belong to the streets. I knew drugs, and stealing and fighting wasn't who I was, but it was who I had become for that time. I knew it wouldn't be permanent. Still, I didn't see a way out.

Though I was in the streets without my biological family, the streets became my family. I had found a safe haven. Miss Effie

Shhh...The Devil is Listening

May was like a guardian angel to us. She took care of us. Effie May and the girls showed me what it meant to be cared for. And because my guard was always up, I kept asking myself the question I expected them to ask, "When are they going to ask something of me?" I was always waiting on them to tell me, "prostitute yourself," something...but they never did.

They showed me more and more affection and though I was guarded, they never forced anything on me.

I asked them questions about sex. I wanted to know how to please a man and if love was supposed to hurt. They were the first ones to make the distinction of the pain in love for me. They said love will hurt your heart, not your body!

We shared many conversations. During one of those conversations, someone asked what a mother's love felt like. My ears perked up because I wanted to know. Many of the women couldn't even answer that question because we didn't know. The one person who did answer said the love from her mother was "indescribable."

When I wasn't around them, I wanted more. Stealing and gang life wasn't enough. I needed something more. Though I felt loved in the streets, I knew I didn't belong in them. I was on a mission to get in and get out of there.

I reminisced often about my God-fearing grandmother. She called me "Pammy." In the streets, I wasn't that little *Pammy* anymore. I was smoking and drinking. I felt like everybody had let me down, so I owed nobody nothing! However, my grandmother was one of the only people that I had maintained lots of respect for. I never wanted her to see me in the state that I was in. I had more respect for my grandmother than I held for my own parents. I hated them, still. I hated my mom; I hated my dad and I hated my brother. For me, it was like, "what can you tell me, you didn't protect me!" They were too busy being concerned about my brother to protect me.

When I did think of family, my grandmother was at the forefront of my mind. I began to recall some of the principles she taught me. Soon, God became a staple in my life. I started to mature. I still couldn't be around my mom, but I began to learn about the power of forgiveness.

By that time, my brother had gotten married and had a baby. Though there were still wounds, the baby, my niece drew us closer. He had been in the streets for a bit too. Many people in the streets didn't know we were siblings. However, when someone tried to come against either of us, we would stand up to protect each other.

Shhh...The Devil is Listening

The gang was still my first family. In fact, when I joined the gang, I had a plan. My plan was to kill my molester, myself. Though, because I was new and hadn't advanced in ranking, I wasn't able to do that right away. After a while, I gained the opportunity and I was going to go forward with it. Killing my molester had actually become an obsession. I wanted to torture the man.

Soon, the opportunity presented itself for me to travel. I was able to go back closer to town.[5] It was a group of us girls. To my surprise, my boyfriend had someone watching my every move. He soon got word about our plan. We had a vocal code set up. At the sound of the code, they would come through the windows and attack. When I arrived at the house to confront him, I walked inside the house. My molester told me that he had been waiting on me. During this time, I had been gone one year and had already celebrated my 17th birthday. His words threw me back. We had everything all planned out, but those words lessened my level of anger. In fact, words began to fail me.

---

[5] Effie May lived on the outskirts of town. It was the same town Pamela lived in with It was in the boonies. It was in a very secluded area. She had no neighbors. The house was away from everything and everybody.

Although, there was one question I wanted to know the answer to more than anything else. I asked him, "Were there anymore that you did like me?" He responded, "I'm waiting on them too." As my original anger returned, somehow the words… "*I FORGIVE YOU*" was somehow uttered from my lips. Each syllable shocked the core of who I had become. My thoughts, now my words and actions totally defied the original agenda! What the hell was happening to me?!

I felt a need to explain: "I'm not forgiving you for you, but I'm forgiving you for me because today I'm being set free from you!"

I remember turning around and walking off the porch. As I reached the last step, I saw my boyfriend coming from around the corner from the side of the house. He said, "I got it from here!" He walked in and told my molester he wanted to talk. The rest of the girls were on the outside. We heard loud screams and hollers come from the inside of that house.

Once my boyfriend came back to me, he said, "If you never thought no one loved you or did anything about it, I want you to know I do, and I've taken care of it!"
It made me reflect back on a conversation we had after we first

started dating and I was still embarrassed about my scars. When we would get ready to indulge in sex, I never got fully undressed. I would wear a long tee-shirt that would come down to my knees. I would make up some excuse about how I was cold or something to diverge the conversation. Though, this one particular time when I was getting out of the shower, he walked in the bathroom. He wanted to know who did this to me. I tried to avoid the question. However, in the gang, we operated with this philosophy, "You don't love me if you don't tell me the truth." I responded, "Well, what are you going to do? I thought, "You don't care about me. Nobody cares about me, what can you do!"

Well, he showed me.

He didn't kill him, but my friends hurt him severely. The beating impacted him and made him remain inside for a while. I remember some of the neighbors saying, "I haven't seen Mr. Neighbor in the while."

I went there to kill him that day. I feel like God needed me more to share this story, so he prevented it that day.

My boyfriend attempted to show his love for me through the encounter with my molester. Somehow, it never made me feel any better. My pain persisted.

I walked away still longing for peace and heroin began to provide that for me. I used it as a relaxer in an effort to be "normal." Later, I started experiencing mental flashes and triggers of my trauma. Next, soaking myself in alcohol plus the heroin became a norm. They were used to numb and normalize my pain.

Once the high wore off, I grew more and more furious about the agony in my life.

One day, I wanted a pity party. It was Friday. So I went and got a whole bunch of heroin. I reached out to a few girlfriends and wanted to buy everyone drinks and celebrate. I told them I was going out of town and I was not coming back. They never knew I that I planned to kill myself that night.

I went back to my apartment and sat on the side of the bed with a .25-millimeter gun. I was tired. I felt like my life wasn't moving anywhere. I could not see anything good coming from me. I was too scared to let anybody in and I was entrenched in the gang life. Stealing had become a key part of my identity. The ones that were supposed to help me hurt me the most. I was hopeless. As I was on the side of the bed, I lifted the loaded gun to my right temple. All sorts of thoughts raced through my head, but the only words that came from my mouth were, "Jesus, help me." I didn't want him to talk me out of what I had planned. I just wanted Him to assist me in taking my own life. Soon, I released the trigger. It jammed. I tried again. The trigger jammed again. "Let's get this over with already," were the thoughts that played again and again in my mind. Frustration began to rise. I got up from the bed and went on the front porch. I had learned to shoot diagonally, instead of straight in the air. I lifted my arms, pointed upward, pulled the trigger and almost instantaneously, shots fired without hesitation.

So, I went back to my bedside and took another stab at killing myself. The gun jammed, again! So, quickly, I went back to the front porch to see if the gun would still work. It worked, without defect. I was in a wrestling match with the gun. I went back and forth to the bedside and the porch three times. By this point, someone had called the local police department to report shots fired. When they arrived, the officer asked if I saw anyone suspicious. I told him I hadn't. I figured; I'd give up the task for the day.

The next day, I went out to the place we were celebrating the day before and some of my same friends were there. One said, "I thought you were leaving!" I told her that I would leave the following day instead.

I owned a .9-millimeter gun. Because I was wearing fake nails, as my finger pressed on the trigger it wouldn't ignite properly. At that point, I bit off the fake nail on my pointer finger and then took an eraser off of a pencil that was laying around. I attempted to use it to apply direct pressure to the trigger, but the eraser kept sliding off the trigger. Nothing was working like I hoped it would! I was so angry!

I had to think of something, I knew would work! I went out and purchased tons of heroin to set myself up for an overdose.

Each time I planned the suicide attempts, I would have my insurance policy laid out on the table. That way, once they found me, they wouldn't have to waste time looking for it. I wanted to have everything set.

I prepared the needle and began shooting in my right arm. I sat there crying and talking to God.

My apartment was upstairs. As I was shooting up, I realized that I had forgot to lock the front door that led to my apartment, but I continued shooting up. I could feel something about to happen. My body started to change inside.

Shhh...The Devil is Listening

Because I was a pretty private person, only those that were close to me were privy to seeing me get high. Sometimes, I would have small gatherings at my place for friends to drink and have a good time. So, on occasions at my place, when I would shoot up with heroin when close friends were there, I was always really discreet. I would stick the needle under my tongue or between my toes or between my fingers. I had some respect for myself. I was what many called a 'hidden' addict. I was also high functioning. Looking at me, you would never know what was happening with me.

As I was shooting up, my girlfriend's husband at the time, happened to stop by while I was in the process of overdosing. I remember me hearing him come up the stairs. He walked in. I'm not sure what he witnessed upon seeing me. I was in a zone but could still hear everything that was going on around me. I could hear the second hand move on his wristwatch. It seemed loud. I could tell my life was slipping away. I remember him smacking me in my face with all his strength. He screamed, "what have you done?" He took my shoulders and started to shake me profusely. I remember him running to the window and hollering downstairs to get the attention of my girlfriend, his wife as she sat in the car. I remember ice cubes being poured all over my body. I remember him saying, "we're going to get you to the hospital." I hadn't responded the whole while, but when he said that, I told him, "no, I don't want to die at the hospital. I'm dying, just get me to my grandmother." He continued to smack me intensely. I don't remember going down the actual stairs, but somehow, I made it to the car. I was in the backseat. I recall being able to see streetlights as the car hurried down the street. I could hear him hollering. He said, "Pam's grandmother please help!" We arrived at her house. They laid me on the floor. He continued to smack me to keep me alert. I believe my grandmother immersed me in a tub. It reminded me of a baptism. I could hear them praying and crying in the background. I felt my life slipping away.

My grandmother could be caught doing one or two things, watching the *700 Club* television show or reading her bible. This day she was reading her bible. As the next morning arrived, the house was quiet. I woke from my slumber. Laying on my grandmother's bed, I looked around and felt a sense of extreme disappointment. I had failed, yet again. My third suicide attempt did not work. As I looked around, the place seemed so serene. Grandma looked at me and gazed into my eyes, her words were like a salve that calmed my frustration. She said, "you're going to be alright." I responded, "no, I'm not!"

Shhh...The Devil is Listening

I lifted myself from the bed. I felt embarrassed that she knew I had attempted to take my own life, but I was still determined to succeed. I was ashamed. I had only wanted to come there to at least die with or near someone who I knew loved me. If I would have died, I wouldn't have had to face her the next morning instead of dying in a lonely hospital. However, since things didn't go as planned, I was livid and ashamed. Now she knew I was on drugs.

I made it to her front door and as I stood there, she muttered these words, "God is going to use you one day." I wasn't convinced. I responded, "How? How will God use somebody like me?" She repeated her original words. And with that, I walked out the door defeated. I thought about how much a failure I was. I thought, "I'm so worthless, that I can't even kill my own self!"

I made my way back to Ms. Effie's, 'safe house'. It was as if God had her waiting on me. She had a one-way bus ticket and information that I would need to check into rehab. Effie May told me to not come back there until I was truly clean. In fact, she said, "I see something in you baby. I just can't put my finger on it. But you're better than this!"

Years later, I understand that she was an angel designed especially for the broken street people, like me, that the churches were so quick to reject. This woman opened her house to 48 women and she never charged a dime for us to stay there. More than that, she showed us how to pray in her flower garden. I learned from her praying to God was an easy task (You just have to talk to him like you talk to another person.) There were things she drilled in our heads. When we went to God in prayer, it was to 'repent and ask God for help on our journey. Every Saturday, she would come around with a brown paper bag and ask us to "give it up." Yes, she made us pay tithes even though we did not attend a church. She didn't care if you were a prostitute, dope dealer, gambler, or even a thief. If you made any kind of money, you were to give God His 10%. If you had a problem with this, you were no longer allowed to hang out at the house.

Effie May believed in me more than I believed in myself. She would say, "Punknella, you're going to make it." But I was still very broken and couldn't see any good coming from me.

I longed for something, but nothing could satisfy me but fighting. When I was fighting, it was when I reminisced about all the things that were done to me. During the fights, I would only envision my molester and not the actual person I was fighting. Then, I began to see myself as a monster because I couldn't explain the intensity of my fighting.

I didn't fit in. Some of the people around me had started to get married and go to college. I had difficulty finding my place. I was stealing and selling drugs. If I was going to steal, I needed to steal big. I remember sitting with Effie May at the kitchen table one day. She put a .22. on the table. Then put a .357 magnum on the table and asked, "If you shoot somebody with either one of these guns, what's going to happen to you? I responded, "I'm going to jail." She said, "Exactly, so go big or stay home." At that point, I stopped stealing small and started stealing big items, items of value.

By this time, I was at a very high rank with my street family. I moved fairly quickly because I was crazy and took no second thought in doing the risky things, they asked of me. I didn't give a damn about anything or anyone!

I began stealing fur coats and getting involved in organized crime. Punknella was a beast and you didn't want to mess around with her!

Eventually, all of this street life was getting old. I was ready for change. I went to rehab. When I was in rehab it was hard because they asked lots of questions. They tried to convince me that they cared about me and my well-being.

They wanted to gain my trust. I couldn't. The streets taught me to trust no one.

I went to many group sessions where we had to share candidly. I made it up in my mind that I would not share anything about myself. For weeks, I just sat staring as the sessions were conducted. I listened but said nothing. However, one day, something changed. A girl told her story during one of the group sessions about why she turned to drugs. She revealed that she had been raped repeatedly for years by a neighbor. She explained that she could no longer cope with what happened to her, but said she wanted to be free. At that moment, my life was starting to change. I wanted to be like her, free. I wanted to be saved. My desire for God grew. I went back to the basics of my life with my grandmothers. She taught me to call on the name of Jesus. I could not quit when things got rough in rehab. I began to open up in rehab about my experiences. Things got very real, my anger and rage were soon exposed. For the first time, I had revealed all the sick shit that had been done to me. Soon, I was able to express how I really felt on the inside. I learned by talking about my past and exposing the ugly truth about my life. I was no longer sitting in the prison in my head. I was finally on my way towards freedom from all my demons. For once, I had a chance to see a glimpse of my future. I could see a little light at the end of the tunnel. As I focused on my sobriety, I didn't worry about what was happening on the outside. I was so caught up in my life, graduation time came swiftly.

I was excited because for the first time in my life, I had completed something that was positive and beneficial for me. I was very proud of myself. Yet, I was still scared because I didn't feel prepared to leave. I was learning about who I was as a free person for the first time in my adult life. I thought about going out and getting high in order to remain in rehab. I vividly remember praying and crying to God for help. Then, a few days before graduation, I learned that there was transitional housing for the graduates.

I had qualified to be able to go there. There we learned about maintaining our sobriety. The more I went to counseling, the more I learned to accept things that was my fault and the things that were outside of my control. I was far from healed, but I was on my way.

I graduated from rehab and I finished my course with transitional housing. I was on my way back home to the X-Rated world that I so vividly remembered. This time, I was determined to stay clean. I did! I had to go back to my street family, but it was hard because drugs were everywhere. However, by God's grace, I made it and I remained clean despite me going back to the street life. I started selling drugs again, for a short time. Yet, selling drugs soon came to an end. When I finished rehab, my only regret was leaving counseling. I enjoyed my sessions but didn't make time for it.

When I came back, I was about 19 years old. I eventually started dating. I was clean. My boyfriend, Ronnie & I had only known each other for 3 months, before we got married. I did it only out of defiance to my parents. We were married at the courthouse. Following the brief ceremony, I took the marriage license to my parents' house and placed it on the table in their room and left. I went home and waited on a phone call. Still, I never uttered a word to them about it. I just left the evidence.

We had $24 to our name to get married. We used $22 to purchase the marriage license and we didn't have money to purchase a ring. So, we used $1 bill for each of us and my girlfriend folded them up and made them into rings for us to exchange with one another.

I started stealing again on a small scale. I started selling drugs again because we were struggling as a new couple.

Still, I had an emptiness. This void ran me to seek out the church. Eventually, I developed a desire for it. I met a woman. She gave me a children's bible because I couldn't read the original version. Then later on my birthday, she gave me a pre-teen bible. This became a training ground for me. My husband became a minister. I was glad for him but was intimidated because I couldn't read out of the original version. I was too embarrassed to bring the pre-teen version to church with me. When I would attend bible study sometimes, they would call me to read out loud. Soon, I would avoid those moments. I thought they were picking on me sometimes, but they didn't know about my learning issues.

To stay out of the limelight, I enjoyed much of the behind the scenes ministry. I would decorate for various events and many people would never know. I couldn't sing, so joining the choir was not an option. I wasn't the smiley type, so ushering wasn't a good position for me. I remember being called out from the pastor about someone complaining about me not smiling.

I moved around to different work. I loved working with the homeless ministry. I could relate to them. When I saw the people smile, it made me smile. I was blessed with the ability to see past their situation and look into their eyes and see the beauty of who they were. Some of the church members would talk about me because I would take time and eat dinner with them. This ministry kept me drawn to the church. I felt good about my contribution.

Though, lots of girls around my age started to build their own families, I kept serving and began to experience peace. I was paying tithes and giving extra for offering. I felt like I was making an important contribution. However, the service to the homeless ended. My light I was starting to develop, started to flicker some. So, I created my own acts of service. I would take food from my own house and find homeless people under the bridge to serve them food. Many of the homeless people that I saw, recognized me from the church. Then, I started helping the elderly in the community. I wanted to do it secretly. I would go grocery shopping for them. Then I would beat on their front doors with a loud bang and go hide in the bushes to watch and see if they received them, then I would leave. One day, I fell into one of the lady's rosebushes. I was all pricked up. It was funny to me though. Deep down, the way I helped them had lots to do with my abuse.

Before my molestation began, I would pick flowers and gift them to people. Often, I would draw pictures and give them to other kids. That stopped. After ripping my pictures, my molester threatened me. He said, "I wish I would catch you giving someone else another picture. I wish I would catch you giving someone another flower! If I see that again, I will cut your fingers off!" I lived with the threat of his confrontation, so I operated in secret, in silence. **Kindness seemed to return**

itself with grief and pain. That drew me away from people, but somehow, I was always found giving away our last.

My husband and I had a beautiful apartment made up of refurbished items that were discovered on the side of the road. When I look back, I can see that God was birthing my talent in me. I treated every piece like it was me; a project. I longed to be rebuilt; to be taken apart and put together again. I took my time on every piece. I dissected each part very gently only to put it back together again. The reconstruction of the trashed furniture represented the essence of who I wanted to be.

Oftentimes, my husband would come home and find most of our food gone because I gifted it to someone less fortunate. Once, our furniture was missing. There were people I felt that needed it more than we did. There were days he went to sit on the couch and turned around and it was missing. Yet, I discovered, the more I gave, the more our family began to reap. There were days, I would open the mailbox to unexpected checks. Once the increases started to show up, the less angry he became. He trusted the God in me. It helped my faith to grow.

Ronnie and I were best friends. You never saw one of us without the other. We were the kind of couple that always communicated, no matter what we were experiencing. I loved my husband very much but not only did I love him; I was in love with him. For the first time in my life, I knew he felt the same way about me.

5

THE FAITH

From the age of 5 until just before my sixteenth birthday, I endured a horrific amount of emotional, psychological and physical abuse at the hands of my "friendly" neighbor. For over a decade, I was forced, threatened and tormented with the shhhh… I was made to keep silent about events that would change my life forever. Bound with this gruesome level of trauma and still able to survive outside a mental institution, is in itself a miracle.

The faith that my grandmother engrained in me is the only thing that kept me. In fact, I often asked God, "Where were you during the rape, the bleach washing, etc.?" The questions became conversation. Because I was so lonely, I learned to talk to God as a little kid. I learned the soothing voice of God. God became my imaginary friend. He began to tell me that the dog that came to lick my wounds was him being there. The molester's dog would always find a way to lick my face, legs, and my hands to let me know that God never left me. God came during each suicidal attempt. The one with the .25 mm, he shut down the trigger. When I went to reach for the .9mm he jammed it again. It was God that even used my friends' husband to come see about me during the heroin overdose attempt. God was there during the fire. The little petite black lady in the hospital was God bringing me peace.

I knew God was with me all along. As a 5-year-old he had become my sole confidant. It was then, I started to learn the sound and tone of his voice and to discern His ways. Still, the abuse left a residue of shame all around me. I was ashamed because of all the body scars. I was ashamed because I never got to give up my own virginity. I was ashamed because I could no longer bare kids. I was ashamed because I thought maybe I wore my skirt too short. Maybe it was something I could have done differently.

Now I know, it wasn't my fault. He was the one with the problem all along. It took the fire and time to process my pain to land at this truth. In fact, the fire humbled me because I was still wounded. I wasn't as hard and cold as I was when I was younger, but I was like my mom's mom, I said anything that came to my mind. I hurt many people with my words. **The fire knocked me down so low that I had no other choice than to finally reach for God again.** I was always aware of who He was, but I didn't often involve Him in my affairs. I needed God because the fire and the abuse impacted me endlessly.

Though my faith is stronger, nevertheless, I have some major challenges that I face still to this day. The difficulty in relationships, the various emotional and mental traumas, and the blurring of purpose would have to be my top few.

Let me explain.

Throughout my life I would reach for people, only for them to let me down. Yet, after the fire, the only thing I salvaged was my husband. However, the Wednesday before the Sunday of the fire, I had planned to leave my husband after learning about a possible issue of infidelity. However, one of my family members talked me out of it. Yet, once the fire happened, the marriage no longer became a priority.

My husband was the same man I had married with paper rings (I kept those rings for the duration of our marriage, but when the fire happened, they were burned) at nineteen years old. We had endured a lot together. Our first years of marriage weren't about love because we barely knew each other. It wasn't about sex; we had already experienced that area. I went from rehab to a marriage. I never really faced my own demons from my past. When I got married, I expected him to help me heal. That was a false expectation because he never possessed the power to help me do so. **I expected him to fix me, when only God could.** I should have never put him in that position. **I was wounded from my past and now wounded from my marriage, but still needed to be healed from my childhood.** Instead of me crying, I began to fight. Fighting was something that I was used to doing. I wanted to be hugged, I wanted to be held. My husband gave me that in the beginning, but it started to stop.

Still, the fact that twenty plus years had passed and we were still together was a miracle. However, because of the intensity of the abuse, it took us a decade to become husband and wife. By the time of our 10th year wedding anniversary, I wanted to do it in the house of God, so we renewed our vows. We both cheated on each other early on in our marriage. We were very young, and we didn't yet take our marriage seriously. We didn't love each other because we didn't know one another. However, at the 10-year mark, things shifted for the better. I grew to love him, and we became best friends.

Our lives became adventurous and we began to do spontaneous travel, but the fire shifted things a lot in our relationship.

I developed post-traumatic stress disorder (PTSD). Every time an ambulance would come out in front of me, I was reminded of the day of the fire. Every time a neighbor would barbecue, I would relive the experience of seeing and smelling the stench of Jessica and Day'Von's severely seared bodies. Friends would tell me to go and get medical help. I avoided this because I was convinced, they would prescribe me medicine. However, because I was an ex-heroin addict, I knew that many people who experienced drug relapses when prescribed medications. I was too scared to risk it.

I somehow thought we would grow closer after the fire, but we grew apart. This represented my breaking point. My dad began to worry about me. The stress and the spirit of death was visible on my life. My hair started to fall out. My eyes were a constant bloodshot red. I was at my lowest. I tried to talk to him about my babies in the fire, but my husband would avoid those conversations.

I experienced a deep paranoia. In the middle of the night I would jump from my sleep out of my bed to run and check the smoke detectors to ensure nothing was burning. I never wanted that to happen again on my watch. **So, after the fire, I didn't have time to fight for a marriage, I was fighting to be sane. I thought I would lose my mind.** Certain sounds would set me off. Those sounds would resemble the fall that Day'Von experienced when his body fell from the top bunk bed into the pit of the fire.

I did go to Christian counseling and God guided me through the entire process. Still, I had carried a .357 magnum in my car ritualistically. Yet, one-point God told me to take it out of the car. Not knowing that God would later direct me to get into my car and His voice would provide me directions on where to drive. Never did I think this would lead me to learn of the secret life my husband was leading.

The pain become too much. I had fought by entire life. I was tired of that way of life.

My husband had become a minister. He was very comfortable doing street level ministry. However, he was told by a pastor at one point that it was time for him to take over a church. However, he rebelled against this because he knew he would touch more people in the streets. So, the man who I once witnessed reading the bible when I made it home, had now turned to the streets.

There were many storms in our marriage. The first storm came when my husband got hurt on his job and was terminated after working his job for several years. Our finances became extremely tight and the stress of bills came on every hand. I was working two jobs trying to do what I could to make things work. At the same time, my mother became gravely ill. I was attempting to work two jobs to take care of my husband on top of making visits to the hospital to take care of my mom during the evenings. Just as I thought I couldn't handle anything else; my mother-in-law became ill. Everything began to take a toll on me physically and mentally. Both of our mothers got better and was soon released from the hospital.

Everything seemed to be going smoothly, and suddenly, my mother took a turn for the worse. She passed away. I turned to my mother-in-law for comfort. The pain from losing her was indescribable. I had many questions about my childhood that I needed her to answer. All of my dreams of ever building a close relationship with my mom, were gone. However, things worsened. One week later, we suddenly lost my mother-in-law to a massive heart attack.

I went into a mode of truly questioning God. I was at a loss for words and filled with great grief. So, I turned to my best friend Chrystal. Chrystal was a minister and truly anointed woman who was closely connected to God. If no one could penetrate my spirit, she could.

I was still working two jobs and Ronnie's injury didn't seem to be getting any better. I started to become bitter towards him. I believed he caused his own injury. I knew he was sick, but no longer cared. My heart was growing cold. I felt like I was no longer his wife, but his mother. As if things couldn't get any worse, Chrystal broke the news that she was diagnosed with cancer. Less than a weeks' time, she was brain dead. I had been waiting on death for a long time, but it never wanted me. I no longer focused on building my marriage but adjusting to the loss that I endured during that five-month stretch.

I was at work that day and was feeling a bit fatigued and overheated. One of my co-workers said I looked pail. I headed home and got in the shower. I woke up on the floor. Later my granddaughter Khloè was able to explain what happened to me. She told me I was crawling from the shower floor and I began to pull on anything that was in my path. I later learned that I was suffering a heart attack.

Shhh...The Devil is Listening

At that point, 3 years had passed since the kids died in the fire. This drove a deeper wedge between Ronnie and me. We were no longer operating as a couple, as husband and wife should. We barely recognized each other. I learned that the death of a child was a pain no drug could numb. As time grew, we had grown so far apart that we could no longer talk without an argument. I didn't want to be in the same room as him. Our marriage had finally died. However, all was not lost because we had our friendship holding us together.

One day, the emotionality of all of the lost hit me. My body began to shut down. Though, I didn't remember much from that day, I do recall smelling the aroma of cheap perfume. It was that day that I decided to get a divorce from my husband. It was all just too much. The lies grew. Leaving early for work and coming home late. Silencing the phone ringers. All of the signs of infidelity were there.

My body was shutting down. After I was released from the hospital, I invited God to help me in this process. I specifically asked God to show me what was happening with my husband. After that prayer, I started to see my husband with various women. I saw hotel receipts, social media messages, etc... I never uttered a word to anyone about what I was experiencing within my marriage. In fact, my friends were shocked when I got a divorce. They had only witnessed me uplifting my husband. They had only witnessed the celebrations for him. I was taught early on that what goes on within a marriage is sacred. It was a space that no one should be allowed into. I held to that truth.

I never wanted to be divorced. However, when the decision came it was after much prayer. I never wanted to be anyone's doormat. I had served that sort of sentence many years prior. That is something that I was never gonna do again. I packed my bags that night and I left.

My husband was very shocked. I had threatened divorce many times, but never made a move. I called my family and asked them to keep Khloé a while. I had never asked for help with her, but I knew it was time for me to start healing.

I filed for divorce on the first of the month and within two weeks it was somehow miraculously finalized. Most people, at least during that time, had to wait 30 days, minimum. I felt God knew I was at a breaking point.

After leaving the house, every time I would come back to it, I felt sick. I knew my husband had committed sin there. The stench would start to sicken me. My now ex-husband moved to the hotel. Then I, along with a few members and leaders from my church, performed a thorough cleaning.

Shhh...The Devil is Listening

Divorce is a loss. I mourned the loss of my husband. Started to miss him being on the other side of the bed. Then I questioned rather or not I made the right decision.

We were together over 20 + years of my life. I was committed to no longer having him ruin any more of my life, so I needed to forgive him quickly.

As time went on, over a 20 + years we began to develop a great friendship, we became best friends. Then we grew into lovers and then we became husband and wife. The lying violated the deep friendship that we had established. This ultimately began to destroy our union.

After the divorce, he lost his job and everything else. So, I invited him to live on the other wing of the house. We worked different shifts; we hardly ever saw one another. Many people, especially from my church ridiculed me for taking him back into the house that we had built together. God tested me because the courts had granted me everything. I was rendered everything, including our granddaughter, Khloé. However, this was a test that I passed. I opened up the house to him. I told him, "whatever is in the refrigerator, you are welcome to it." My kindness almost destroyed him. Outsiders called me stupid. I remained focused because I believed in the blessings that God allowed me in losing nothing from the divorce. It was a difficult thing to do. I wanted him to pay for the damage and pain that he had caused to me in the adultery. However, God graced me to stick it out.

If I could do it all over again, I wouldn't change a thing. Though brief, their presence in my life gave me the gift that I never thought I would have, they gave me family. Day'Von gave me a reason to fight for a better life. His mom gave me a reason to fight for her because it made her get out of the streets because I knew how it would end. All of them, Jessica, Day'Von and Khloé were only a part of my life, because of my husband.

Though, my ex-husband and I have settled our relationship and have become good friends, and excellent co-parents for Khloè, I still have trouble gaining new relationships. For me, everyone starts out as my enemy and through trial and error, they grow into friendships.

This is a direct drawback from the abuse. The neighbors—the babysitters and my molester, all presented themselves as friendly. They said kind words and did 'friendly' things, yet they assaulted my body and murdered my memories of what childhood should have reflected.

Shhh...The Devil is Listening

Although, the physical acts of molestation have ended, the emotional turmoil had a lasting impact on me. As I grew older, for decades when it was time to eat, the taste of blood would flood my mouth. I soon learned it was a mental experience I suffered from the abuse. Some of my friends and family would sometime notice that when I would drink or eat something, I would often make a frown. If they made a dish for me, frequently they would ask, "Was it bad?" Often too embarrassed to explain, I would switch the subject.

During one of my episodes, my mind would go back to the instance where I mistakenly put my hand on my mouth after trying to comfort my inflamed vagina. Some mornings I would have attacks and it would seem like somebody had poured blood all into my mouth.

After forty years, in 2016,[6] I was finally freed from this intense trauma.

Another level of emotional trauma I experienced from the abuse was becoming numb and emotionless. When I was younger, I figured, "Nobody was there to wipe my tears. Nobody cared enough so I began to get hard. Nobody put a cold rag on me and told me it would be alright. Nobody patted

---

[6] I went on sixty-day religious fast in an effort to become more whole. At the end of that fasting time and period of consecration, I no longer experienced this trauma.

me on the back." So, I became hard. Especially with the gang life, it was nothing for me to go to a house and kick the door down with the entire family waiting behind it.

Then more recently I knew I still needed to be healed in this area. My girlfriend's young son fell off the bed while jumping and hit his head on the side of the dresser. Blood shot everywhere. Both, he and his mother cried hysterically from the time it happened almost until the time we left the hospital. I was there to witness it all from start to finish. Then, when I went home at the end of the night, I became concerned about how disengaged I was in regard to being emotionless about the entire ordeal. It was then that I knew, there was a problem.

My emotions were lifeless. In fact, the only time I cried was when Day'Von died in the fire. I remember when I first got Day'Von, I would put sticky notes in various places throughout the house to remind to extend love towards him. I didn't know how to give love outside of this because I had never truly received it before that time. So, when he died, I cried profusely. I read books on how to show love and how to be a mother. Those level of emotions had been stolen from me.

Up until a few months ago, I was reminded every day when I took my clothes off as a nearly 50-year-old woman, of the sin

Shhh...The Devil is Listening

that was committed against me when I was 5. Though I am still working daily on emotional healing, I made a choice to have the surgeon remove the physical stains of the molestation from my body. This was an intense process. After a long search, less than a year ago, I was able to find a surgeon that would remove the cigarette burn scars from my body. With a total of three major surgeries, I was able to remove all the burns. It was then that my journey began.

I had developed an insane amount of tolerance for pain. The nurses were shocked at how much I could endure. The surgery was intense. After my first surgery, I wore a wound vacuum for more than 3 months. I had to carry a long tube and purse like canister over my shoulder. The nurses came twice a week to my house to change the wound out. There was a long tube that ran from the opening of my wounds to the canister that linked fluids and infected parts of my flesh. At first everything seemed fine. However, emotionally, my mind started again to relive my childhood trauma. This same smell that reeked from my vagina as a five-year-old was the same one that I smelled that day. I learned; the smell was evidence that a life-threatening infection had set in my body.

It took me back to my 5-year-old self. I sobbed and mourned for her. No one knew what I endured and therefore my wounds were only treated with bleach.

Yet, that day it was embarrassing because though I had nurses around me, I knew that the foul odor belonged to me because Khloè told me. The foul odor was from the fluids that excreted from the wounds of my flesh.

I only took antibiotics to clear the infection and over the counter Tylenol to assist with the pain. The wound was 1 foot wide and 8 inches deep.

The doctors warned me that I would possibly go through a mourning process to rid my body of the wounds from my past. The scars have been with me for over 40 years. Losing them was a death in a way. My brain had to realize that the burns were gone. This was similar to the grieving process my brain and body was forced to experience (as an acceptance process) after "receiving" the burns.

Though the scars have been removed, the memories of how they got there are forever tattooed on my soul…in my mind and my emotions.

Nevertheless, the surgeries have been an active step in my process to wholeness.

Moreover, the greatest source of pain for me has been in the unknown. This was a part of my daily war. As I constantly learn to live with what happened to me, I still grapple with my purpose and identity.

After the molestation, I believe my whole path got rerouted. I often wondered what I would have been. For the small to the more complex questions about the person I was destined to become. I never had time to consider things like, my favorite color or the music I truly enjoy. I often sit and wonder how my life would have turned out had my journey not been intercepted by such evil. Would I had ever made it to college? Would I have richer friendships and relationships in general? Would I have ever needed to go to counseling? Would I... I wonder. Did I have a purpose in life that the evil impeded upon? If so, is it possible to regain consciousness or is it too late for me? Who was I designed to be? Who was I originally?

You see, I don't have an answer to these questions.

This hurt, is something my faith has yet to make peace with.

PAMELA MCKINNEY

6

THE FORMATION

With this book, I want to let someone know that they are not alone on this journey. Molestation isolates you. You feel alone. You feel unacknowledged. You feel like the only one. With this book, I hope to create a larger community for those molested, especially those who experienced pain to the extent I did.

In 2017, I thought I found someone else like me. She told me she had been burned in between her legs with a cigarette too. I gained a little peace that day. When asking more details about the events, facts didn't measure up well.

I do know, molestation impacts each person differently. For instance, my only grade school friend had been molested by her stepdad.

As a result, she became very timid. For me, I became a fighter. I did not glory in my aggression; I made a conscious decision that no one was going to be given the chance to hurt me anymore. I hid behind the pain and allowed the violent Pam to come out. "If you hit me, I'm hitting you back! If you cut me, I'm cutting you back. If you pull a gun out on me, I'm pulling one out back." This was what my life had become.

Consequently, I ended the relationship with my friend. Her timidity began to rule her personality and because my life had become so hard, I was afraid that I would damage her further. I ended the friendship.

As a result, I now know that not everyone is called to join forces. However, I believe there are a countless number of people that need to know we are in this together.

In fact, when I stood in front of my molester that day to seek revenge, things started to shift in me. When he mentioned the other victims, I instantly started to rack my brain to think about the possibilities of who else there could be. Who else's innocence was snatched? Who else?

Shhh...The Devil is Listening

At that point, the searching began. I went on a trek to stop the damage to other kids that he took. It was at that point I decided I would not be silent anymore. Though, it took nearly thirty years for that decision to become the action of this book. I am still committed to that cause.

Contrary to popular belief, most survivors don't tell their story easily. In fact, we shy away from the spotlight. Many of us carry our pain in the crevices of our bodies and the recesses of our minds, only. However, for me, with the fire, God thrusted open something in me that can never be silenced again.

I have come to the point of accepting that this is the path God knew I could walk. This acceptance does not make this task easy. My prayer is the fire that pushed me, would allow me to get a group of survivors in formation to impact change between ourselves and eventually with the rest of the world.

PAMELA MCKINNEY

7

THE FORGIVING

Thank you so much for taking the time to read about some of my journey through abuse and my journey towards healing. A great majority of events in my story happened several decades ago. I want to take the time to briefly share where things in my life are currently.

When you're molested, everyone loses something of their own. I lost my ability to have children. Other people lost something else. Though it was intense, I always knew that God never left me. In losing the ability to bare children, God gifted me Khloè and Day'Von. As you've read, Khloé survived the fire.

Khloè has been a part of my family since she was 3 weeks old. She is currently nine years old. This season is all about Khloé, ensuring she gets through life on the smoothest path possible. I love Khloé. She is a sweet girl. Our relationship is amazing. I am very open to her about my life and struggles. We've grown strong in our bond and she is the joy of my life. I work every day to become her greatest role model. She speaks of her brother frequently. And we have worked diligently to keep his memory alive.

In fact, we started an organization in honor of her brother called *Day'Von's Blessing*. This is an organization that I established after the fire, to give to children and families who are less fortunate. Day'Von had a beautiful smile. So, during the holiday seasons we hope to bring smiles to families by paying the cost of their Christmas lay-a-ways.

Khloé and my ex-husband are still really close. He picks her up from the school bus each day. We participate in activities together frequently. Khloé understands that we are family.

As for me, because throughout my life I experienced lots of neglect and abandonment at the hands of adults, I am extremely watchful. I'm still learning to extend trust towards adults. However, I am much more trusting towards children.

I've finally grown to a place of receiving love. However, I still have a slight guard up. If someone says they love me, they have to show me first. Nevertheless, I'm learning to love me and focus more directly on my healing. I have held off on entertaining new relationships as I'm giving myself a chance on two very important things:

    1) Love myself unconditionally, and

    2) Walk into the purpose God has designed for me.

I truly believe that once I enter into my purpose fully, everything that I'm desiring from God will already be waiting on me. I've done so many things in my life, but these are two things I've never experienced.

In addition, I have been more open about sharing the details of my horrific journey. I even plan a yearly conference-in my area called "Broken and Not Destroyed." The conference has been a regional platform I have used to share my story about abuse. Each year when I'm preparing for the conference I go on an intense period of fasting. During those times, God wakes me up in the middle of the night and reveal to me various mysteries about my life, about my past, about my abuse. My body has started to change for the better. I lost weight and my mentality is shifting in a positive direction.

My dad is now in his mid-seventies. Our relationship is well. In fact, I finally told him the truth about my journey. While he failed to respond verbally, his face filled with anger, hurt, and hatred. Because I know Daddy, if my molester were still alive, my dad would have murdered him with his bare hands. After our conversation, I feel like Dad has a greater understanding of who I am. While I struggle some, I am no longer angry at him for not knowing I was being molested by someone we both trusted. Dad is hurt because he feels like he didn't save his baby from the monster that he thought was his friend.

My mom died in October of 2006, at the age of 56. She was sick for a while and suffered some. I would try and buy her love with gifts. I'm not sure that it worked. I often wondered if my mom was still alive would she love me now. That, I will never know. However, I wish I would have gotten to know my mother a lot more. I love my mother and I needed my mother both physically and mentally. As a woman, I carried so many secrets that needed to be told to my mother. However, my bitterness towards her would not let me open up to her about the horrific things I experienced as a child. I didn't reach out to my mother for answers. My molester 'took' my mother away from me as a child and replaced her with a whole bunch of lies in my mind.

Shhh...The Devil is Listening

To tell a child that their mother doesn't truly love them is incredibly awful. I've finally accepted the things that I cannot change. I've also started the journey of forgiveness.

For the people that may have known what was being done to me. I forgive you.

I miss love, but I often ask, how can I miss something I've never experienced.

In all, God has given me more than I ever imagined. The crippling impact of the intensity of my childhood tried it's best to take me out! It nearly succeeded. However, God built within me a supernatural fortitude to withstand some of the most atrocious actions committed against a 37-lb, five-year-old.

I still have a few psychological bruises here and there, but I made it.

YOU CAN TOO!

PAMELA MCKINNEY

Final Note

TO MY MOLESTOR:

Even though you would beat me when I would respond to your question about whether or not I loved my mother, my father or brother...you may have thought you won. As a child, you had power over me. You hoped that I remained quiet, but I want you to know that there was this man that was sitting high and looking low down on me. He put grace and favor on my life and all around me. Everything that was taken from me He's giving it all back! I have God in my life and can truly say that I LOVE my mother, my Daddy, and my Brother, Eric. This is a great gift!

For the record, I forgive you and pray that God has mercy on your very soul.

Now, I can begin to close this chapter of my life because the demons that had me bound have been now been exposed. Your actions sought to destroy me, yet today I can stand strong and say, despite all the things you did to me, and took away: I WON! I'm wounded, but I WON! I am released. I'm free from you!

I came through some very ugly stuff, but as the scripture in Ezekiel reads, I, *"You became very beautiful and rose to be a queen."* For this, I thank Jesus!

~Pamela

PAMELA MCKINNEY

Shhh...The Devil is Listening
NOTES

_____

_____

NOTES

Shhh...The Devil is Listening
NOTES

NOTES

Shhh...The Devil is Listening
NOTES

NOTES

Shhh...The Devil is Listening

CONTACT AUTHOR

If you experienced anything similar to what I experienced or know anybody that experienced what I did, I want to hear from you! I need your help. I want to connect with you!

Please email below for booking signing or speaking engagements.

Please contact me via directly via email at
ChatwithPamNOW@gmail.com.

DO YOU WANT TO WRITE A BOOK?

Contact our publisher at

www.drnesintl.com

www.ingramcontent.com/pod-product-compliance
Lightning Source LLC
Chambersburg PA
CBHW031347160426
43196CB00007B/762